U.S. Fish & Wildlife Service

Adaptive Harvest Management

2006 Hunting Season

MIGRATORY BIRD HUNTING AND CONSERVATION STAMP

$15

Ross' Goose

Void after June 30, 2007

U.S. DEPARTMENT OF THE INTERIOR

Adaptive Harvest Management
2006 Hunting Season

PREFACE

The process of setting waterfowl hunting regulations is conducted annually in the United States (Blohm 1989). This process involves a number of meetings where the status of waterfowl is reviewed by the agencies responsible for setting hunting regulations. In addition, the U.S. Fish and Wildlife Service (USFWS) publishes proposed regulations in the *Federal Register* to allow public comment. This document is part of a series of reports intended to support development of harvest regulations for the 2006 hunting season. Specifically, this report is intended to provide waterfowl managers and the public with information about the use of adaptive harvest management (AHM) for setting duck-hunting regulations in the United States. This report provides the most current data, analyses, and decision-making protocols. However, adaptive management is a dynamic process and some information presented in this report will differ from that in previous reports.

Citation: U.S. Fish and Wildlife Service. 2006. Adaptive Harvest Management: 2006 Hunting Season. U.S. Dept. Interior, Washington, D.C. 45pp.

ACKNOWLEDGMENTS

A working group comprised of representatives from the USFWS, the Canadian Wildlife Service (CWS), and the four Flyway Councils (Appendix A) was established in 1992 to review the scientific basis for managing waterfowl harvests. The working group, supported by technical experts from the waterfowl management and research community, subsequently proposed a framework for adaptive harvest management, which was first implemented in 1995. The USFWS expresses its gratitude to the AHM Working Group and to the many other individuals, organizations, and agencies that have contributed to the development and implementation of AHM.

This report was prepared by the USFWS Division of Migratory Bird Management. F. A. Johnson and G. S. Boomer were the principal authors. Individuals that provided essential information or otherwise assisted with report preparation were D. Case (D.J. Case & Assoc.), M. Conroy (U.S. Geological Survey [USGS]), E. Cooch (Cornell University), P. Garrettson (USFWS), W. Harvey (Maryland Dept. of Natural Resources), R. Raftovich (USFWS), E. Reed (Canadian Wildlife Service), K. Richkus (USFWS), J. Royle (USGS), M. Runge (USGS), J. Serie, (USFWS), S. Sheaffer (Cornell University), and K. Wilkins (USFWS). Comments regarding this document should be sent to the Chief, Division of Migratory Bird Management - USFWS, 4401 North Fairfax Drive, MS MSP-4107, Arlington, VA 22203.

TABLE OF CONTENTS

This report and others regarding Adaptive Harvest Management are available online at
http://migratorybirds.fws.gov

EXECUTIVE SUMMARY

In 1995 the U.S. Fish and Wildlife Service (USFWS) implemented the Adaptive Harvest Management (AHM) program for setting duck hunting regulations in the United States. The AHM approach provides a framework for making objective decisions in the face of incomplete knowledge concerning waterfowl population dynamics and regulatory impacts.

The original AHM protocol was based solely on the dynamics of mid-continent mallards, but efforts are being made to account for mallards breeding eastward and westward of the mid-continent region. The challenge for managers is to vary hunting regulations among Flyways in a manner that recognizes each Flyway's unique breeding-ground derivation of mallards. For the 2006 hunting season, the USFWS will continue to consider a regulatory choice for the Atlantic Flyway that depends exclusively on the status of eastern mallards. The prescribed regulatory choice for the Mississippi, Central, and Pacific Flyways continues to depend exclusively on the status of mid-continent mallards. Investigations of the dynamics of western mallards (and their potential effect on regulations in the West) are continuing and the USFWS is not yet prepared to recommend an AHM protocol for this mallard stock.

The mallard population models that are the basis for prescribing hunting regulations were revised extensively in 2002. These revised models account for an apparent positive bias in estimates of survival and reproductive rates, and also allow for alternative hypotheses concerning the effects of harvest and the environment in regulating population size. Model-specific weights reflect the relative confidence in alternative hypotheses, and are updated annually using comparisons of predicted and observed population sizes. For mid-continent mallards, current model weights favor the weakly density-dependent reproductive hypothesis (91%). Evidence for the additive-mortality hypothesis remains equivocal (58%). For eastern mallards, current model weights favor the strongly density-dependent reproductive hypothesis (65%). By consensus, hunting mortality is assumed to be additive in eastern mallards.

For the 2006 hunting season, the USFWS is continuing to consider the same regulatory alternatives as last year. The nature of the restrictive, moderate, and liberal alternatives has remained essentially unchanged since 1997, except that extended framework dates have been offered in the moderate and liberal alternatives since 2002. Also, at the request of the Flyway Councils in 2003 the USFWS agreed to exclude closed duck-hunting seasons from the AHM protocol when the breeding-population size of mid-continent mallards is >5.5 million (traditional survey area plus the Great Lakes region).

Harvest rates associated with each of the regulatory alternatives are predicted using Bayesian statistical methods. Essentially, the idea is to use historical information to develop initial harvest-rate predictions, to make regulatory decisions based on those predictions, and then to observe realized harvest rates. Those observed harvest rates, in turn, are used to update the predictions. Using this approach, predictions of harvest rates of mallards under the regulatory alternatives have been updated based on band-reporting rate studies conducted since 1998. Estimated harvest rates from the 2002-2005 liberal hunting seasons have averaged 0.12 (SD = 0.01) and 0.14 (SD = 0.01) for adult male mid-continent and eastern mallards, respectively. The estimated marginal effect of framework-date extensions has been an increase in harvest rate of 0.012 (SD = 0.008) and 0.006 (SD = 0.010) for mid-continent and eastern mallards, respectively.

Optimal regulatory strategies for the 2006 hunting season were calculated using: (1) harvest-management objectives specific to each mallard stock; (2) the 2006 regulatory alternatives; and (3) current population models and associated weights for mid-continent and eastern mallards. Based on this year's survey results of 7.86 million mid-continent mallards (traditional survey area plus MN, WI, and MI), 4.45 million ponds in Prairie Canada, and 899 thousand eastern mallards, the optimal regulatory choice for all four Flyways is the liberal alternative.

BACKGROUND

The annual process of setting duck-hunting regulations in the United States is based on a system of resource monitoring, data analyses, and rule-making (Blohm 1989). Each year, monitoring activities such as aerial surveys and hunter questionnaires provide information on population size, habitat conditions, and harvest levels. Data collected from this monitoring program are analyzed each year, and proposals for duck-hunting regulations are developed by the Flyway Councils, States, and USFWS. After extensive public review, the USFWS announces regulatory guidelines within which States can set their hunting seasons.

In 1995, the USFWS adopted the concept of adaptive resource management (Walters 1986) for regulating duck harvests in the United States. This approach explicitly recognizes that the consequences of hunting regulations cannot be predicted with certainty, and provides a framework for making objective decisions in the face of that uncertainty (Williams and Johnson 1995). Inherent in the adaptive approach is an awareness that management performance can be maximized only if regulatory effects can be predicted reliably. Thus, adaptive management relies on an iterative cycle of monitoring, assessment, and decision-making to clarify the relationships among hunting regulations, harvests, and waterfowl abundance.

In regulating waterfowl harvests, managers face four fundamental sources of uncertainty (Nichols et al. 1995, Johnson et al. 1996, Williams et al. 1996):

(1) environmental variation - the temporal and spatial variation in weather conditions and other key features of waterfowl habitat; an example is the annual change in the number of ponds in the Prairie Pothole Region, where water conditions influence duck reproductive success;

(2) partial controllability - the ability of managers to control harvest only within limits; the harvest resulting from a particular set of hunting regulations cannot be predicted with certainty because of variation in weather conditions, timing of migration, hunter effort, and other factors;

(3) partial observability - the ability to estimate key population attributes (e.g., population size, reproductive rate, harvest) only within the precision afforded by extant monitoring programs; and

(4) structural uncertainty - an incomplete understanding of biological processes; a familiar example is the long-standing debate about whether harvest is additive to other sources of mortality or whether populations compensate for hunting losses through reduced natural mortality. Structural uncertainty increases contentiousness in the decision-making process and decreases the extent to which managers can meet long-term conservation goals.

AHM was developed as a systematic process for dealing objectively with these uncertainties. The key components of AHM include (Johnson et al. 1993, Williams and Johnson 1995):

(1) a limited number of regulatory alternatives, which describe Flyway-specific season lengths, bag limits, and framework dates;

(2) a set of population models describing various hypotheses about the effects of harvest and environmental factors on waterfowl abundance;

(3) a measure of reliability (probability or "weight") for each population model; and

(4) a mathematical description of the objective(s) of harvest management (i.e., an "objective function"), by which alternative regulatory strategies can be compared.

These components are used in a stochastic optimization procedure to derive a regulatory strategy. A regulatory strategy specifies the optimal regulatory choice, with respect to the stated management objectives, for each possible combination of breeding population size, environmental conditions, and model weights (Johnson et al. 1997). The setting of annual hunting regulations then involves an iterative process:

(1) each year, an optimal regulatory choice is identified based on resource and environmental conditions, and on current model weights;

(2) after the regulatory decision is made, model-specific predictions for subsequent breeding population size are determined;

(3) when monitoring data become available, model weights are increased to the extent that observations of population size agree with predictions, and decreased to the extent that they disagree; and

(4) the new model weights are used to start another iteration of the process.

By iteratively updating model weights and optimizing regulatory choices, the process should eventually identify which model is the best overall predictor of changes in population abundance. The process is optimal in the sense that it provides the regulatory choice each year necessary to maximize management performance. It is adaptive in the sense that the harvest strategy "evolves" to account for new knowledge generated by a comparison of predicted and observed population sizes.

MALLARD STOCKS AND FLYWAY MANAGEMENT

Since its inception AHM has focused on the population dynamics and harvest potential of mallards, especially those breeding in mid-continent North America. Mallards constitute a large portion of the total U.S. duck harvest, and traditionally have been a reliable indicator of the status of many other species. As management capabilities have grown, there has been increasing interest in the ecology and management of breeding mallards that occur outside the mid-continent region. Geographic differences in the reproduction, mortality, and migrations of mallard stocks suggest that there may be corresponding differences in optimal levels of sport harvest. The ability to regulate harvests of mallards originating from various breeding areas is complicated, however, by the fact that a large degree of mixing occurs during the hunting season. The challenge for managers, then, is to vary hunting regulations among Flyways in a manner that recognizes each Flyway's unique breeding-ground derivation of mallards. Of course, no Flyway receives mallards exclusively from one breeding area, and so Flyway-specific harvest strategies ideally must account for multiple breeding stocks that are exposed to a common harvest.

The optimization procedures used in AHM can account for breeding populations of mallards beyond the mid-continent region, and for the manner in which these ducks distribute themselves among the Flyways during the hunting season. An optimal approach would allow for Flyway-specific regulatory strategies, which in a sense represent for each Flyway an average of the optimal harvest strategies for each contributing breeding stock, weighted by the relative size of each stock in the fall flight. This joint optimization of multiple mallard stocks requires: (1) models of population dynamics for all recognized stocks of mallards; (2) an objective function that accounts for harvest-management goals for all mallard stocks in the aggregate; and (3) decision rules allowing Flyway-specific regulatory choices.

Joint optimization of multiple stocks presents many challenges in terms of population modeling, parameter estimation, and computation of regulatory strategies. These challenges cannot always be overcome due to limitations in monitoring and assessment programs and in access to sufficient computing resources. In some cases, it may be possible to impose constraints or assumptions that simplify the problem. Although sub-optimal by design, these constrained regulatory strategies may perform nearly as well as those that are optimal, particularly in cases where breeding stocks differ little in their ability to support harvest, where Flyways do not receive significant numbers of birds from more than one breeding stock, or where management outcomes are highly uncertain.

Currently, two stocks of mallards are officially recognized for the purposes of AHM (Fig. 1). We continue to use a constrained approach to the optimization of these stock's harvest, whereby the Atlantic Flyway regulatory strategy is based exclusively on the status of eastern mallards, and the regulatory strategy for the remaining Flyways is based exclusively on the status of mid-continent mallards. This approach has been determined to perform nearly as well as a joint-optimization approach because mixing of the two stocks during the hunting season is limited.

5

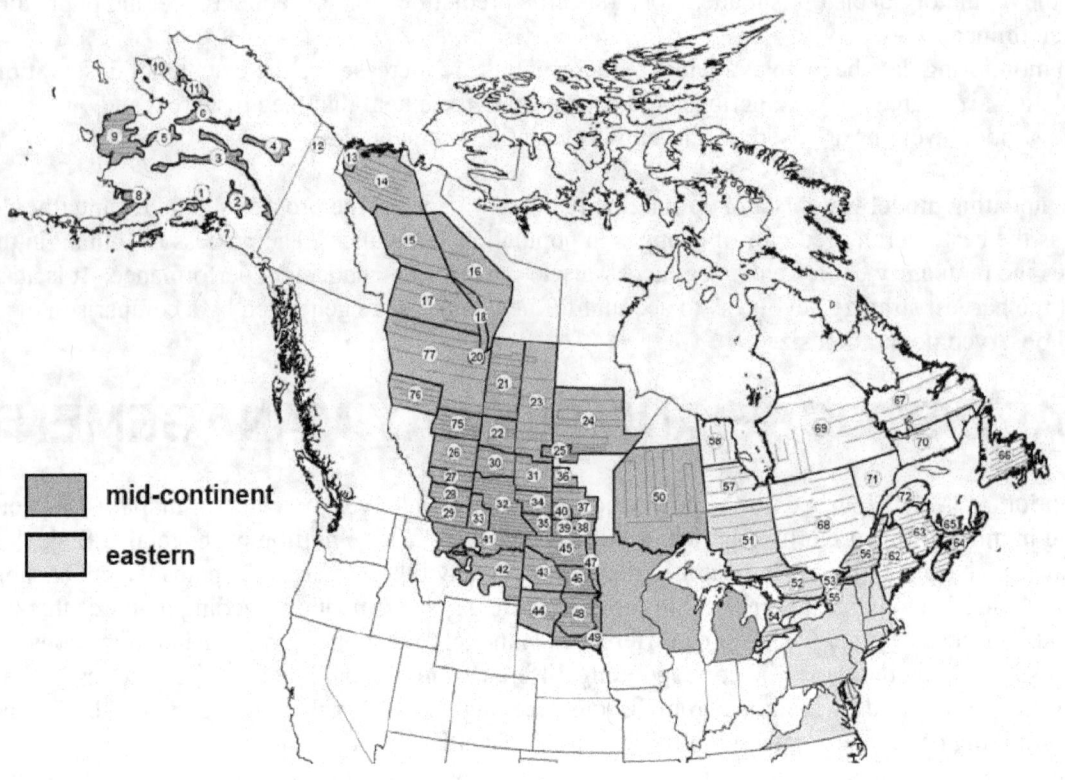

Fig 1. Survey areas currently assigned to the mid-continent and eastern stocks of mallards for the purposes of AHM. Delineation of the western-mallard stock is pending further review and development of population models and monitoring programs.

MALLARD POPULATION DYNAMICS

Mid-continent Mallards

Population size.--For the purposes of AHM, mid-continent mallards currently are defined as those breeding in federal survey strata 1-18, 20-50, and 75-77 (i.e., the "traditional" survey area), and in Minnesota, Wisconsin, and Michigan. Estimates of the abundance of this mid-continent population are available only since 1992 (Table 1, Fig. 2).

Population models.-In 2002 we extensively revised the set of alternative models describing the population dynamics of mid-continent mallards (Runge et al. 2002, USFWS 2002). Collectively, the models express uncertainty (or disagreement) about whether harvest is an additive or compensatory form of mortality (Burnham et al. 1984), and whether the reproductive process is weakly or strongly density-dependent (i.e., the degree to which reproductive rates decline with increasing population size).

Table 1. Estimates (N) and standard errors (SE) of mallards (in millions) in spring in the traditional survey area (strata 1-18, 20-50, and 75-77) and the states of Minnesota, Wisconsin, and Michigan.

Year	Traditional surveys		State surveys		Total	
	N	SE	N	SE	N	SE
1992	5.9761	0.2410	0.9946	0.1597	6.9706	0.2891
1993	5.7083	0.2089	0.9347	0.1457	6.6430	0.2547
1994	6.9801	0.2828	1.1505	0.1163	8.1306	0.3058
1995	8.2694	0.2875	1.1214	0.1965	9.3908	0.3482
1996	7.9413	0.2629	1.0251	0.1443	8.9664	0.2999
1997	9.9397	0.3085	1.0777	0.1445	11.0174	0.3407
1998	9.6404	0.3016	1.1224	0.1792	10.7628	0.3508
1999	10.8057	0.3445	1.0591	0.2122	11.8648	0.4046
2000	9.4702	0.2902	1.2350	0.1761	10.7052	0.3395
2001	7.9040	0.2269	0.8622	0.1086	8.7662	0.2516
2002	7.5037	0.2465	1.0820	0.1152	8.5857	0.2721
2003	7.9497	0.2673	0.8360	0.0734	8.7857	0.2772
2004	7.4253	0.2820	0.9333	0.0748	8.3586	0.2917
2005	6.7553	0.2808	0.7862	0.0650	7.5415	0.2883
2006	7.2765	0.2237	0.5881	0.4645	7.8646	0.2284

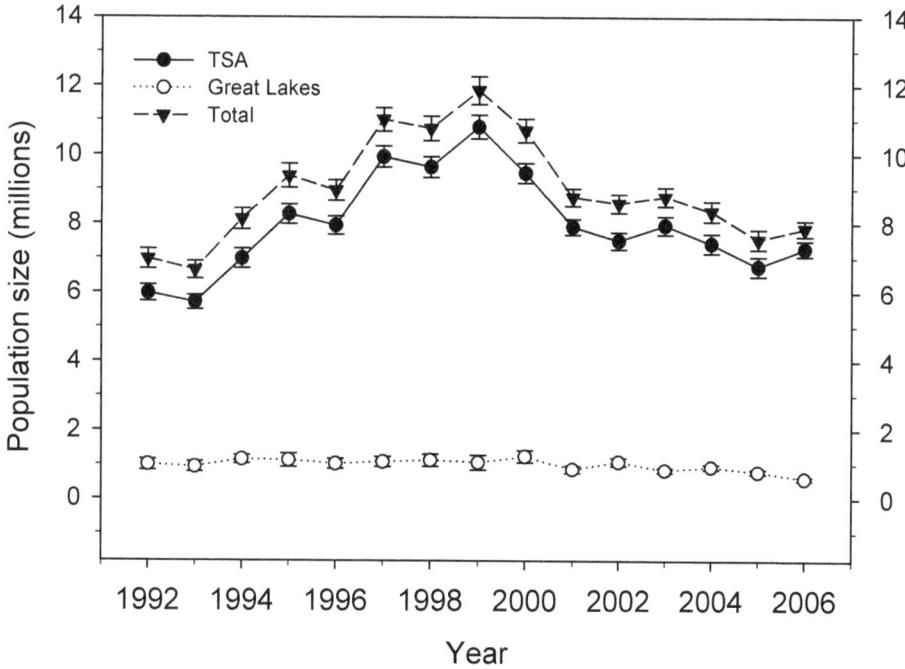

Fig. 2. Population estimates of mid-continent mallards in the traditional survey area (TSA) and the Great Lakes region. Error bars represent one standard error.

7

All population models for mid-continent mallards share a common "balance equation" to predict changes in breeding-population size as a function of annual survival and reproductive rates:

$$N_{t+1} = N_t \left(m S_{t,AM} + \left(1 - m\right)\left(S_{t,AF} + R_t \left(S_{t,JF} + S_{t,JM}\, \phi_F^{sum} / \phi_M^{sum}\right)\right)\right)$$

where:
N = breeding population size,
m = proportion of males in the breeding population,
S_{AM}, S_{AF}, S_{JF}, and S_{JM} = survival rates of adult males, adult females, young females, and young males, respectively,
R = reproductive rate, defined as the fall age ratio of females,
$\phi_F^{sum} / \phi_M^{sum}$ = the ratio of female (F) to male (M) summer survival, and
t = year.

We assumed that m and $\phi_F^{sum} / \phi_M^{sum}$ are fixed and known. We also assumed, based in part on information provided by Blohm et al. (1987), the ratio of female to male summer survival was equivalent to the ratio of annual survival rates in the absence of harvest. Based on this assumption, we estimated $\phi_F^{sum} / \phi_M^{sum} = 0.897$. To estimate m we expressed the balance equation in matrix form:

$$\begin{bmatrix} N_{t+1,AM} \\ N_{t+1,AF} \end{bmatrix} = \begin{bmatrix} S_{AM} & RS_{JM}\, \phi_F^{sum} / \phi_M^{sum} \\ 0 & S_{AF} + RS_{JF} \end{bmatrix} \begin{bmatrix} N_{t,AM} \\ N_{t,AF} \end{bmatrix}$$

and substituted the constant ratio of summer survival and means of estimated survival and reproductive rates. The right eigenvector of the transition matrix is the stable sex structure that the breeding population eventually would attain with these constant demographic rates. This eigenvector yielded an estimate of $m = 0.5246$.

Using estimates of annual survival and reproductive rates, the balance equation for mid-continent mallards over-predicted observed population sizes by 10.8% on average. The source of the bias is unknown, so we modified the balance equation to eliminate the bias by adjusting both survival and reproductive rates:

$$N_{t+1} = \gamma_S N_t \left(m S_{t,AM} + \left(1 - m\right)\left(S_{t,AF} + \gamma_R R_t \left(S_{t,JF} + S_{t,JM}\, \phi_F^{sum} / \phi_M^{sum}\right)\right)\right)$$

where γ denotes the bias-correction factors for survival (S) and reproduction (R). We used a least squares approach to estimate $\gamma_S = 0.9479$ and $\gamma_R = 0.8620$.

Survival process. – We considered two alternative hypotheses for the relationship between annual survival and harvest rates. For both models, we assumed that survival in the absence of harvest was the same for adults and young of the same sex. In the model where harvest mortality is additive to natural mortality:

$$S_{t,sex,age} = s_{0,sex}^A \left(1 - K_{t,sex,age}\right)$$

and in the model where changes in natural mortality compensate for harvest losses (up to some threshold):

$$S_{t,sex,age} = \begin{cases} s_{0,sex}^C & \text{if } K_{t,sex,age} \leq 1 - s_{0,sex}^C \\ 1 - K_{t,sex,age} & \text{if } K_{t,sex,age} > 1 - s_{0,sex}^C \end{cases}$$

where s_0 = survival in the absence of harvest under the additive (*A*) or compensatory (*C*) model, and *K* = harvest rate adjusted for crippling loss (20%, Anderson and Burnham 1976). We averaged estimates of s_0 across banding reference areas by weighting by breeding-population size. For the additive model, s_0 = 0.7896 and 0.6886 for males and females, respectively. For the compensatory model, s_0 = 0.6467 and 0.5965 for males and females, respectively. These estimates may seem counterintuitive because survival in the absence of harvest should be the same for both models. However, estimating a common (but still sex-specific) s_0 for both models leads to alternative models that do not fit available band-recovery data equally well. More importantly, it suggests that the greatest uncertainty about survival rates is when harvest rate is within the realm of experience. By allowing s_0 to differ between additive and compensatory models, we acknowledge that the greatest uncertainty about survival rate is its value in the absence of harvest (i.e., where we have no experience).

Reproductive process.–Annual reproductive rates were estimated from age ratios in the harvest of females, corrected using a constant estimate of differential vulnerability. Predictor variables were the number of ponds in May in Prairie Canada (*P*, in millions) and the size of the breeding population (*N*, in millions). We estimated the best-fitting linear model, and then calculated the 80% confidence ellipsoid for all model parameters. We chose the two points on this ellipsoid with the largest and smallest values for the effect of breeding-population size, and generated a weakly density-dependent model:

$$R_t = 0.7166 + 0.1083P_t - 0.0373N_t$$

and a strongly density-dependent model:

$$R_t = 1.1390 + 0.1376P_t - 0.1131N_t$$

Pond dynamics.–We modeled annual variation in Canadian pond numbers as a first-order autoregressive process. The estimated model was:

$$P_{t+1} = 2.2127 + 0.3420P_t + \varepsilon_t$$

where ponds are in millions and ε_t is normally distributed with mean = 0 and variance = 1.2567.

Variance of prediction errors.–Using the balance equation and sub-models described above, predictions of breeding-population size in year *t+1* depend only on specification of population size, pond numbers, and harvest rate in year *t*. For the period in which comparisons were possible, we compared these predictions with observed population sizes.

We estimated the prediction-error variance by setting:

$$e_t = \ln\left(N_t^{obs}\right) - \ln\left(N_t^{pre}\right)$$

$$\text{then assuming} \quad e_t \sim N\left(0, \sigma^2\right)$$

$$\text{and estimating} \quad \hat{\sigma}^2 = \sum_t \left[\ln\left(N_t^{obs}\right) - \ln\left(N_t^{pre}\right)\right]^2 \Big/ (n-1)$$

where *obs* and *pre* are observed and predicted population sizes (in millions), respectively, and *n* = the number of years being compared. We were concerned about a variance estimate that was too small, either by chance or because the number of years in which comparisons were possible was small. Therefore, we calculated the upper 80% confidence limit for σ^2 based on a Chi-squared distribution for each combination of the alternative survival and reproductive sub-models, and then averaged them. The final estimate of σ^2 was 0.0243, equivalent to a coefficient of variation of about 17%.

Model implications.--The set of alternative population models suggests that carrying capacity (average population size in the absence of harvest) for an average number of Canadian ponds is somewhere between about 6 and 16 million mallards. The population model with additive hunting mortality and weakly density-dependent recruitment (SaRw) leads to the most conservative harvest strategy, whereas the model with compensatory hunting mortality and strongly density-dependent recruitment (ScRs) leads to the most liberal strategy. The other two models (SaRs and ScRw) lead to strategies that are intermediate between these extremes. Under the models with compensatory hunting mortality (ScRs and ScRw), the optimal strategy is to have a liberal regulation regardless of population size or number of ponds because at harvest rates achieved under the liberal alternative, harvest has no effect on population size. Under the strongly density-dependent model (ScRs), the density-dependence regulates the population and keeps it within narrow bounds. Under the weakly density-dependent model (ScRw), the density-dependence does not exert as strong a regulatory effect, and the population size fluctuates more.

Model weights.--Model weights are calculated as Bayesian probabilities, reflecting the relative ability of the individual alternative models to predict observed changes in population size. The Bayesian probability for each model is a function of the model's previous (or prior) weight and the likelihood of the observed population size under that model. We used Bayes' theorem to calculate model weights from a comparison of predicted and observed population sizes for the years 1996-2004, starting with equal model weights in 1995. For the purposes of updating, we predicted breeding-population size in the traditional survey area in year $t + 1$, from breeding-population size, Canadian ponds, and harvest rates in year t.

Model weights changed little until all models under-predicted the change in population size from 1998 to 1999, perhaps indicating there is a significant factor affecting population dynamics that is absent from all four models (Fig. 3). Throughout the period of updating model weights, there has been no clear preference for either the additive (58%) or compensatory (42%) mortality models. For most of the time frame, model weights have strongly favored the weakly density-dependent (91%) reproductive model over the strongly density-dependent (9%) one. The reader is cautioned, however, that models can sometimes make reliable predictions of population size for reasons having little to do with the biological hypotheses expressed therein (Johnson et al. 2002*b*).

Inclusion of mallards in the Great Lakes region.--Model development originally did not include mallards breeding in the states of Wisconsin, Minnesota, and Michigan, primarily because full data sets were not available from these areas to permit the necessary analysis. However, mallards in the Great Lakes region have been included in the mid-continent mallard AHM protocol since 1997 by assuming that population dynamics for these mallards are similar to those in the traditional survey area. Based on that assumption, predictions of breeding population size are scaled to reflect inclusion of mallards in the Great Lakes region. From 1992 through 2006, when population estimates were available for all three states, the average proportion of the total mid-continent mallard population that was in the Great Lakes region was 0.1117 (SD = 0.0200). We assumed a normal distribution with these parameter values to make the conversion between the traditional survey area and total breeding-population size.

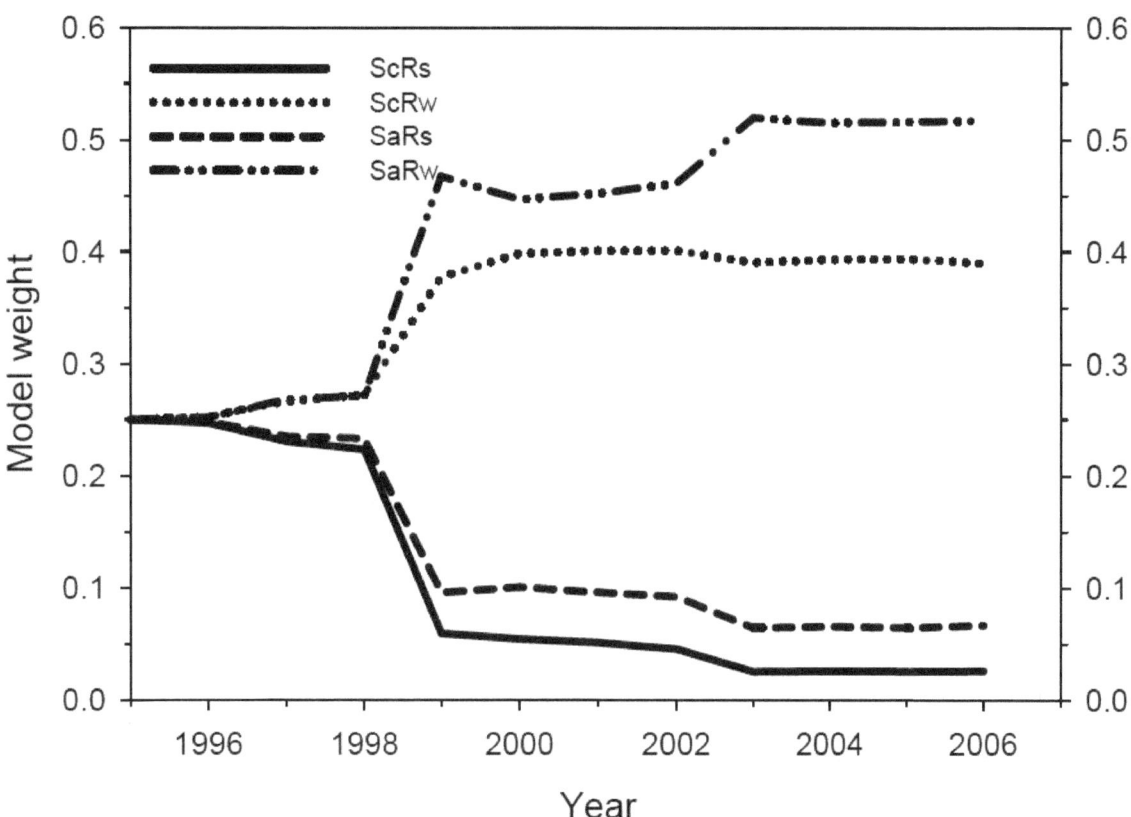

Fig 3. Weights for models of mid-continent mallards (ScRs = compensatory mortality and strongly density-dependent reproduction, ScRw = compensatory mortality and weakly density-dependent reproduction, SaRs = additive mortality and strongly density-dependent reproduction, and SaRw = additive mortality and weakly density-dependent reproduction). Model weights were assumed to be equal in 1995.

Eastern Mallards

Population size.--For purposes of AHM, eastern mallards are defined as those breeding in southern Ontario and Quebec (federal survey strata 51-54 and 56) and in the northeastern U.S. (state plot surveys; Heusman and Sauer 2000) (see Fig. 1). Estimates of population size have varied from 856 thousand to 1.1 million since 1990, with the majority of the population accounted for in the northeastern U.S. (Table 3, Fig. 4). The reader is cautioned that these estimates differ from those reported in the USFWS annual waterfowl trend and status reports, which include composite estimates based on more fixed-wing strata in eastern Canada and helicopter surveys conducted by CWS.

Population models.–We also revised the population models for eastern mallards in 2002 (Johnson et al. 2002a, USFWS 2002). The current set of six models: (1) relies solely on federal and state waterfowl surveys (rather than the Breeding Bird Survey) to estimate abundance; (2) allows for the possibility of a positive bias in estimates of survival or reproductive rates; (3) incorporates competing hypotheses of strongly and weakly density-dependent reproduction; and (4) assumes that hunting mortality is additive to other sources of mortality.

Table 3. Estimates (N) and associated standard errors (SE) of mallards (in thousands) in spring in the northeastern U.S. (state plot surveys) and eastern Canada (federal survey strata 51-54 and 56).

Year	State surveys		Federal surveys		Total	
	N	SE	N	SE	N	SE
1990	665.1	78.3	190.7	47.2	855.8	91.4
1991	779.2	88.3	152.8	33.7	932.0	94.5
1992	562.2	47.9	320.3	53.0	882.5	71.5
1993	683.1	49.7	292.1	48.2	975.2	69.3
1994	853.1	62.7	219.5	28.2	1072.5	68.7
1995	862.8	70.2	184.4	40.0	1047.2	80.9
1996	848.4	61.1	283.1	55.7	1131.5	82.6
1997	795.1	49.6	212.1	39.6	1007.2	63.4
1998	775.1	49.7	263.8	67.2	1038.9	83.6
1999	879.7	60.2	212.5	36.9	1092.2	70.6
2000	757.8	48.5	132.3	26.4	890.0	55.2
2001	807.5	51.4	200.2	35.6	1007.7	62.5
2002	834.1	56.2	171.3	30.0	1005.4	63.8
2003	731.8	47.0	308.3	55.4	1040.1	72.6
2004	809.1	51.8	301.5	53.3	1110.7	74.3
2005	753.6	53.6	293.4	53.1	1047.0	75.5
2006	725.2	47.9	174.0	28.4	899.2	55.7

As with mid-continent mallards, all population models for eastern mallards share a common balance equation to predict changes in breeding-population size as a function of annual survival and reproductive rates:

$$N_{t+1} = N_t \cdot \left(\left(p \cdot S_t^{am} \right) + \left((1-p) \cdot S_t^{af} \right) + \left(p \cdot \left(A_t^m / d \right) \cdot S_t^{ym} \right) + \left(p \cdot \left(A_t^m / d \right) \cdot \psi \cdot S_t^{yf} \right) \right)$$

where:
N = breeding-population size,
p = proportion of males in the breeding population,
S^{am}, S^{af}, S^{ym}, and S^{yf} = survival rates of adult males, adult females, young males, and young females, respectively,
A^m = ratio of young males to adult males in the harvest,
d = ratio of young male to adult male direct recovery rates,
ψ = the ratio of male to female summer survival, and t = year.

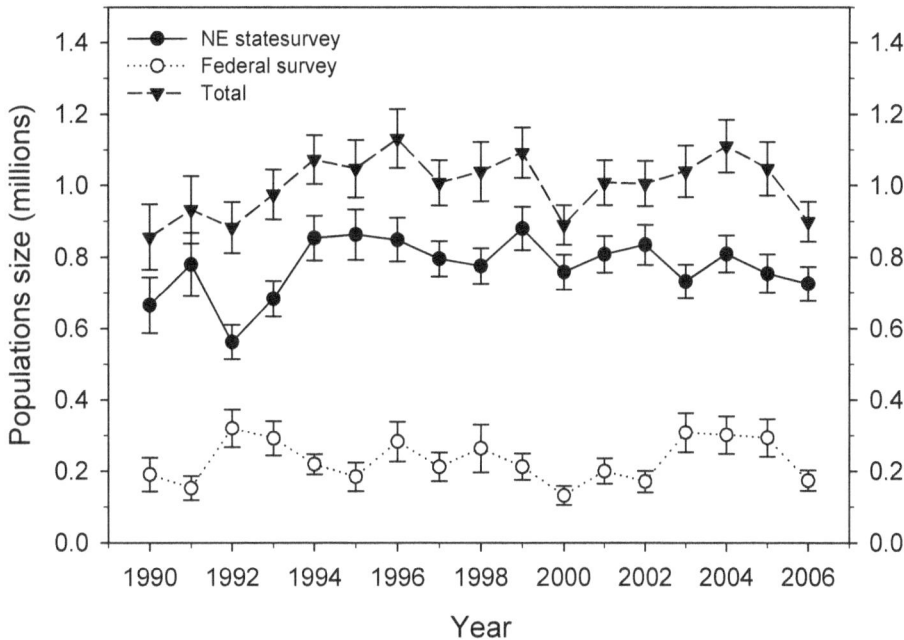

Fig. 4. Population estimates of eastern mallards in the northeastern U.S. (NE state survey) and in federal surveys in southern Ontario and Quebec. Error bars represent one standard error.

In this balance equation, we assume that p, d, and ψ are fixed and known. The parameter ψ is necessary to account for the difference in anniversary date between the breeding-population survey (May) and the survival and reproductive rate estimates (August). This model also assumes that the sex ratio of fledged young is 1:1; hence A^m/d appears twice in the balance equation. We estimated $d = 1.043$ as the median ratio of young:adult male band-recovery rates in those states from which wing receipts were obtained. We estimated $\psi = 1.216$ by regressing through the origin estimates of male survival against female survival in the absence of harvest, assuming that differences in natural mortality between males and females occur principally in summer. To estimate p, we used a population projection matrix of the form:

$$\begin{bmatrix} M_{t+1} \\ F_{t+1} \end{bmatrix} = \begin{bmatrix} S^{am} + \left(A^m/d\right)\cdot S^{ym} & 0 \\ \left(A^m/d\right)\cdot \psi \cdot S^{yf} & S^{af} \end{bmatrix} \cdot \begin{bmatrix} M_t \\ F_t \end{bmatrix}$$

where M and F are the relative number of males and females in the breeding populations, respectively. To parameterize the projection matrix we used average annual survival rate and age ratio estimates, and the estimates of d and ψ provided above. The right eigenvector of the projection matrix is the stable proportion of males and females the breeding population eventually would attain in the face of constant demographic rates. This eigenvector yielded an estimate of $p = 0.544$.

We also attempted to determine whether estimates of survival and reproductive rates were unbiased. We relied on the balance equation provided above, except that we included additional parameters to correct for any bias that might exist. Because we were unsure of the source(s) of potential bias, we alternatively assumed that any bias resided solely in survival rates:

$$N_{t+1} = N_t \cdot \Omega \cdot \left(\left(p \cdot S_t^{am}\right) + \left((1-p)\cdot S_t^{af}\right) + \left(p \cdot \left(A_t^m/d\right)\cdot S_t^{ym}\right) + \left(p \cdot \left(A_t^m/d\right)\cdot \psi \cdot S_t^{yf}\right) \right)$$

(where Ω is the bias-correction factor for survival rates), or solely in reproductive rates:

$$N_{t+1} = N_t \cdot \left(\left(p \cdot S_t^{am} \right) + \left((1-p) \cdot S_t^{af} \right) + \left(p \cdot \alpha \cdot \left(A_t^m / d \right) \cdot S_t^{ym} \right) + \left(p \cdot \alpha \cdot \left(A_t^m / d \right) \cdot \psi \cdot S_t^{yf} \right) \right)$$

(where α is the bias-correction factor for reproductive rates). We estimated Ω and α by determining the values of these parameters that minimized the sum of squared differences between observed and predicted population sizes. Based on this analysis, $\Omega = 0.836$ and $\alpha = 0.701$, suggesting a positive bias in survival or reproductive rates. However, because of the limited number of years available for comparing observed and predicted population sizes, we also retained the balance equation that assumes estimates of survival and reproductive rates are unbiased.

Survival process.–For purposes of AHM, annual survival rates must be predicted based on the specification of regulation-specific harvest rates (and perhaps on other uncontrolled factors). Annual survival for each age (i) and sex (j) class under a given regulatory alternative is:

$$S_t^{i,j} = \overline{\theta}^{\,j} \cdot \left(1 - \frac{\left(h_t^{am} \cdot v^{i,j} \right)}{(1-c)} \right)$$

where:

S = annual survival,

$\overline{\theta}^{\,j}$ = mean survival from natural causes,

h^{am} = harvest rate of adult males, and

v = harvest vulnerability relative to adult males,

c = rate of crippling (unretrieved harvest).

This model assumes that annual variation in survival is due solely to variation in harvest rates, that relative harvest vulnerability of the different age-sex classes is fixed and known, and that survival from natural causes is fixed at its sample mean. We estimated $\overline{\theta}^{\,j} = 0.7307$ and 0.5950 for males and females, respectively.

Reproductive process.–As with survival, annual reproductive rates must be predicted in advance of setting regulations. We relied on the apparent relationship between breeding-population size and reproductive rates:

$$R_t = a \cdot \exp(b \cdot N_t)$$

where R_t is the reproductive rate (i.e., A_t^m / d), N_t is breeding-population size in millions, and a and b are model parameters. The least-squares parameter estimates were $a = 2.508$ and $b = -0.875$. Because of both the importance and uncertainty of the relationship between population size and reproduction, we specified two alternative models in which the slope (b) was fixed at the least-squares estimate ± one standard error, and in which the intercepts (a) were subsequently re-estimated. This provided alternative hypotheses of strongly density-dependent ($a = 4.154$, $b = -1.377$) and weakly density-dependent reproduction ($a = 1.518$, $b = -0.373$).

Variance of prediction errors.--Using the balance equations and sub-models provided above, predictions of breeding-population size in year $t+1$ depend only on the specification of a regulatory alternative and on an estimate of population size in year t. For the period in which comparisons were possible (1991-96), we were interested in how well these predictions corresponded with observed population sizes. In making these comparisons, we were primarily concerned with how well the bias-corrected balance equations and reproductive and survival sub-models performed. Therefore, we relied on estimates of harvest rates rather than regulations as model inputs.

We estimated the prediction-error variance by setting:

$$e_t = \ln\left(N_t^{obs}\right) - \ln\left(N_t^{pre}\right)$$

$$\text{then assuming} \quad e_t \sim N\left(0, \sigma^2\right)$$

$$\text{and estimating} \quad \hat{\sigma}^2 = \sum_t \left[\ln\left(N_t^{obs}\right) - \ln\left(N_t^{pre}\right)\right]^2 \Big/ n$$

where *obs* and *pre* are observed and predicted population sizes (in millions), respectively, and $n = 6$.

Variance estimates were similar regardless of whether we assumed that the bias was in reproductive rates or in survival, or whether we assumed that reproduction was strongly or weakly density-dependent. Thus, we averaged variance estimates to provide a final estimate of $\sigma^2 = 0.006$, which is equivalent to a coefficient of variation (*CV*) of 8.0%. We were concerned, however, about the small number of years available for estimating this variance. Therefore, we estimated an 80% confidence interval for σ^2 based on a Chi-squared distribution and used the upper limit for $\sigma^2 = 0.018$ (i.e., $CV = 14.5\%$) to express the additional uncertainty about the magnitude of prediction errors attributable to potentially important environmental effects not expressed by the models.

Model implications.--Model-specific regulatory strategies based on the hypothesis of weakly density-dependent reproduction are considerably more conservative than those based on the hypothesis of strongly density-dependent reproduction. The three models with weakly density-dependent reproduction suggest a carrying capacity (i.e., average population size in the absence of harvest) >2.0 million mallards, and prescribe extremely restrictive regulations for population size <1.0 million. The three models with strongly density-dependent reproduction suggest a carrying capacity of about 1.5 million mallards, and prescribe liberal regulations for population sizes >300 thousand. Optimal regulatory strategies are relatively insensitive to whether models include a bias correction or not. All model-specific regulatory strategies are "knife-edged," meaning that large differences in the optimal regulatory choice can be precipitated by only small changes in breeding-population size. This result is at least partially due to the small differences in predicted harvest rates among the current regulatory alternatives (see the section on Regulatory Alternatives later in this report).

Model weights.—We used Bayes' theorem to calculate model weights from a comparison of predicted and observed population sizes for the years 1996-2006. We calculated weights for the alternative models based on an assumption of equal model weights in 1996 (the last year data was used to develop most model components) and on estimates of year-specific harvest rates (Appendix B). There is no single model that is clearly favored over the others at the end of the time frame, although collectively the models with strongly density-dependent reproduction (65%) are better predictors of changes in population size than those with weak density dependence (35%) (Fig. 5). In addition, there is substantial evidence of bias in extant estimates of survival and/or reproductive rates (99%).

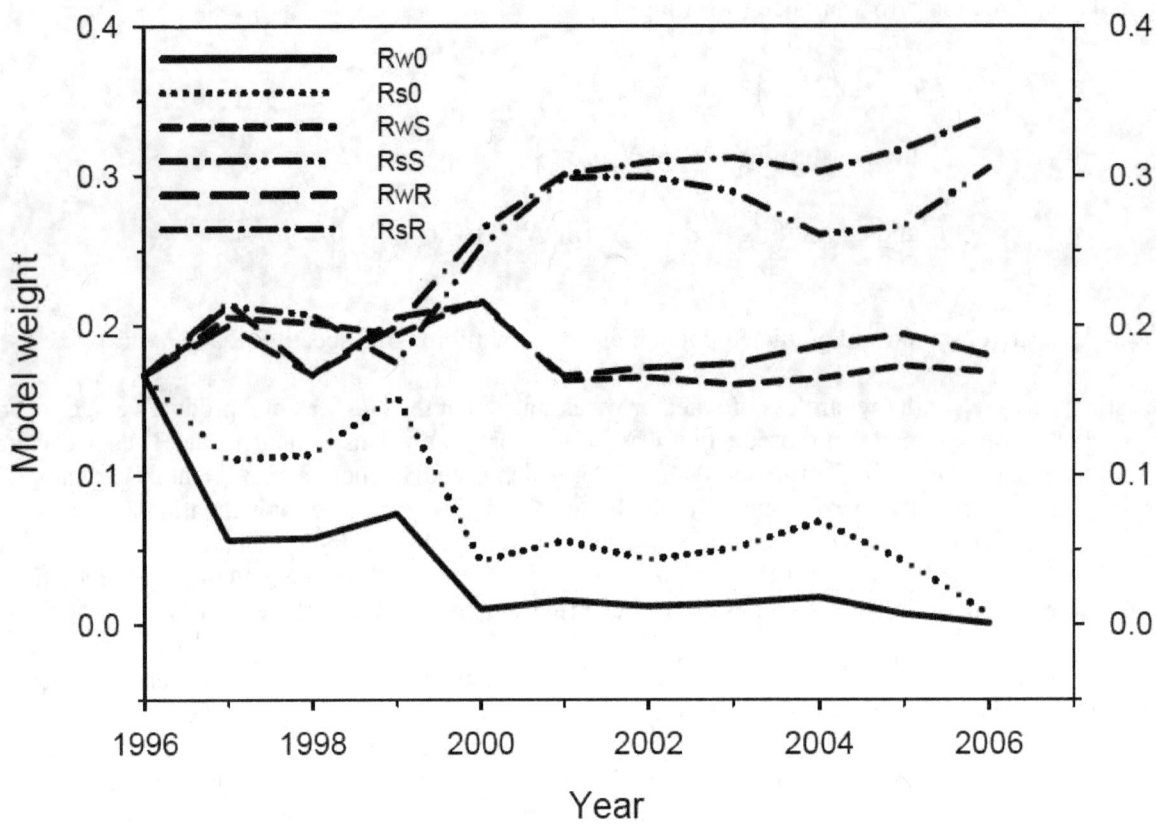

Fig. 5. Weights for models of eastern mallards (Rw0 = weak density-dependent reproduction and no model bias, Rs0 = strong -dependent reproduction and no model bias, RwS = weak density-dependent reproduction and biased survival rates, RsS = strong density-dependent reproduction and biased survival rates, RwR = weak density-dependent reproduction and biased reproductive ates, and RsR = strong density-dependent reproduction and biased reproductive rates). Model weights were assumed to be equal in 1996.

Western Mallards

Substantial numbers of mallards occur in the states of the Pacific Flyway (including Alaska), British Columbia, and the Yukon Territory during the breeding season. The distribution of these mallards during fall and winter is centered in the Pacific Flyway (Munro and Kimball 1982). Unfortunately, data-collection programs for understanding and monitoring the dynamics of this mallard stock are highly fragmented in both time and space. This makes it difficult to aggregate monitoring instruments in a way that can be used to reliably model this stock's dynamics and, thus, to establish criteria for regulatory decision-making under AHM. Another complicating factor is that federal survey strata 1-12 in Alaska and the Yukon are within the current geographic bounds of mid-continent mallards. The AHM Working Group is continuing its investigations of western mallards and while it is not prepared to recommend an AHM protocol at this time, progress is being made on a number of issues:

Breeding populations surveys – The development of AHM for western mallards continues to present technical challenges that make implementation much more difficult than with either mid-continent or eastern mallards. In particular, we remain concerned about our ability to reliably determine changes in the population size of western mallards based on a collection of surveys conducted independently by Pacific Flyway States and the Province of British Columbia. These surveys tend to vary in design and intensity, and in some cases lack measures of precision (i.e., sampling error). For example, methods for estimating mallard abundance in British Columbia are still in the development and evaluation phase, and there are as yet unanswered questions about how mallard abundance will be determined there on an operational basis. Helicopters are currently being evaluated for use in surveys that eventually could cover the majority of key waterfowl habitats in British Columbia.

During the last year we reviewed extant surveys to determine their adequacy for supporting a western-mallard AHM protocol. We were principally interested in whether the surveys: (a) estimate total birds (rather than breeding pairs); (b) have a sound sampling design (and SEs available); (c) consider imperfect detection of birds; and (d) require data augmentation (i.e., filling missing years). Based on these criteria, Alaska, California, and Oregon were selected for modeling purposes. These three states likely harbor about 75% of the western-mallard breeding population (Fig. 6). Nonetheless, this geographic focus is temporary until such time that surveys in other areas can be brought up to similar standards and an adequate record of population estimates is available for analysis.

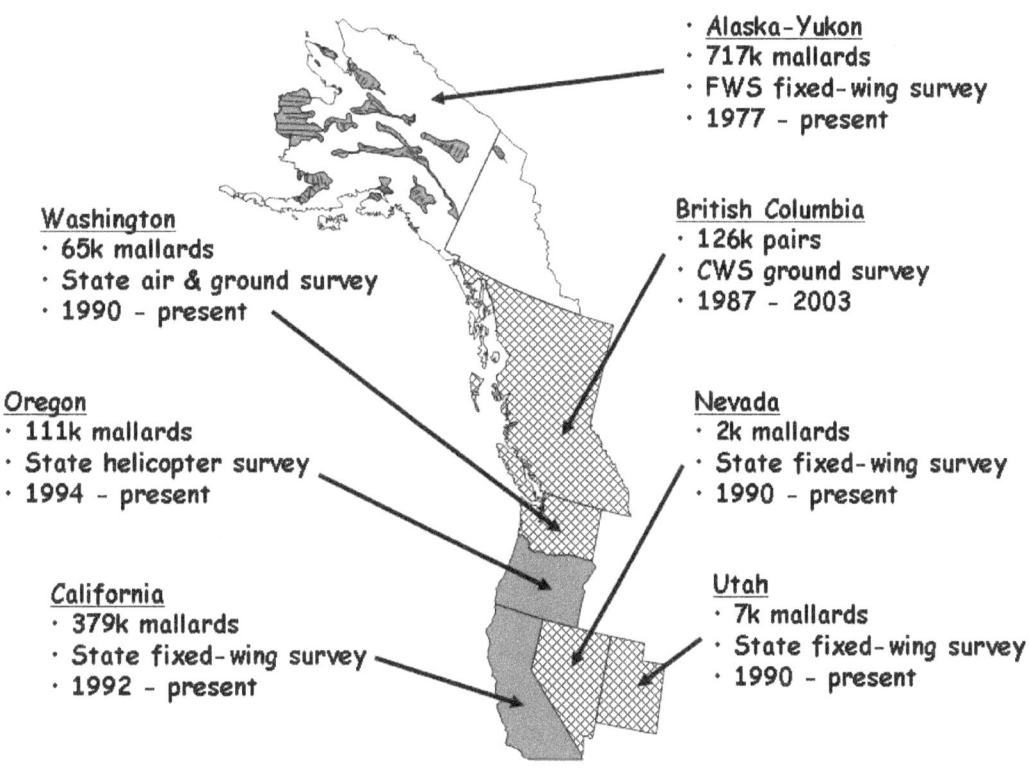

Fig. 6. Status of surveys in the range of western mallards. States with solid shading represent those that currently are being used to model western-mallard population dynamics.

17

Population modeling – For modeling purposes we were hesitant to pool Alaska mallards with those in California and Oregon because of differing population trajectories (Fig. 7), and because we believed it likely that different environmental driving variables were at play during the breeding season in northern and southern latitudes. Mallards banded in Alaska and in Californian/Oregon also had different recovery distributions, suggesting that these two groups of mallards may be subject to differences in mortality rates during the non-breeding season. The separation of western mallards into northern and southern groups is for exploratory purposes. It remains unclear whether the dynamics of these two groups are different enough to be meaningful in a harvest-management context, especially given that many of these birds are subject to a common hunting season.

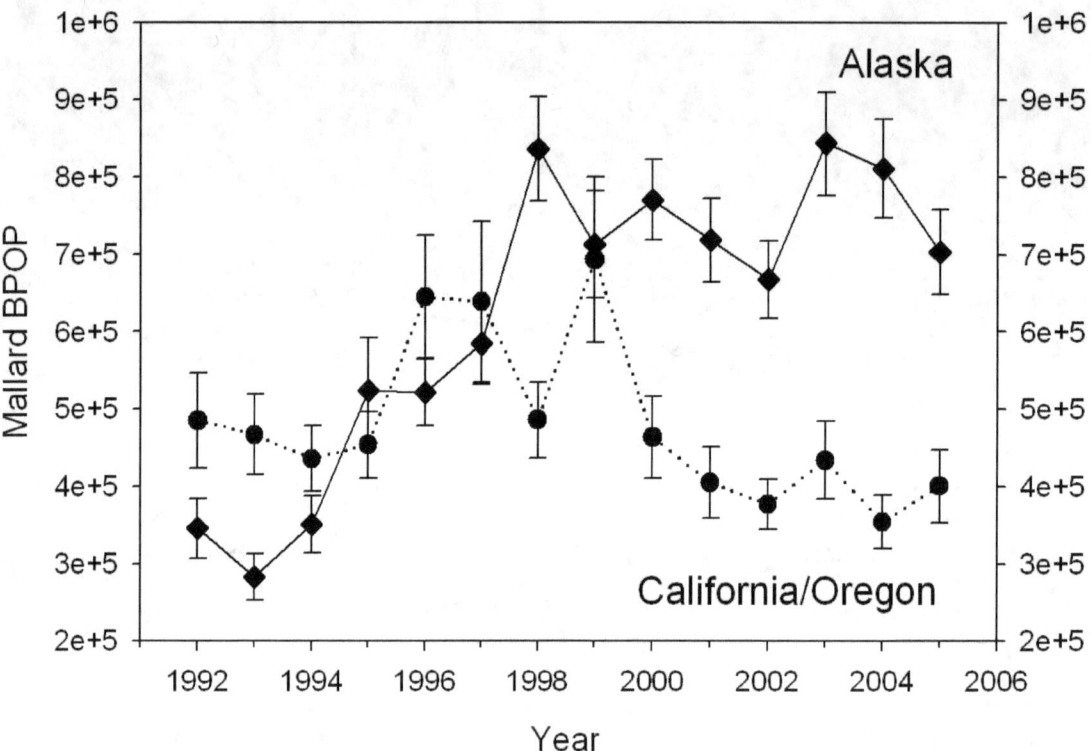

Fig. 7. Population estimates of two groups of western mallards. Surveys were not conducted in Oregon in 1992, 1993, and 2001 so we imputed estimates based on the correlation between estimates from Oregon and California. Error bars represent one standard error.

We used a discrete logistic model to characterize population dynamics because it requires a minimum of data to parameterize. The traditional approach of constructing a population balance equation (i.e., that used for mid-continent and eastern mallards) was deemed impractical because of the paucity of banding data to estimate survival rates and because of the difficulty of estimating reproductive rates from a collection of wings aggregated from several mallard stocks. The logistic model took the form:

$$N_{t+1} = N_t + N_t r \left(1 - \frac{N_t}{K}\right) - \alpha_t \left(N_t + N_t r \left(1 - \frac{N_t}{K}\right)\right) + \sigma^2$$

$$where \quad \alpha_t = \frac{h_t^{AM}}{(1-c)} d$$

and where: N = breeding-population size, r = the intrinsic rate of population growth, K = carrying capacity, h^{AM} =

adult-male harvest rate, c = crippling loss, d = a scaling factor, and σ^2 = process error.

As model inputs, we used breeding population estimates (derived from breeding surveys) and harvest rates of adult males (derived from band-recovery data corrected for reporting rates). We assumed a 20% crippling loss and scaled adult-male harvest rates (d) to represent a harvest-rate for the population as a whole. The magnitude of d depends on the differential vulnerability of the age-sex cohorts, as well as their relative abundance in the population. Based on values from better understood mallard stocks we specified $d = 1.4$, but also explicitly allowed for considerable variation in this parameter throughout the analyses.

The model we used assumes that both the Alaska and California-Oregon breeding stocks are closed. While this is a tenuous assumption, breeding-ground fidelity is difficult to investigate using dead recoveries of banded birds, even where large samples are available from all stocks of interest (in this case including mid-continent mallards). Low fidelity could lead to poor model fit; however, this lack of fit should be absorbed in the process-error term. The logistic model also assumes density-dependent growth, but does not specify whether it occurs in the mortality process, the reproductive process, or both. However, some assumptions about the seasonality of events had to be assumed in order to reconcile the different timing of population surveys and preseason banding.

We used a "state-space model" that allows the partitioning of observation error, which is specified by the sampling error of population estimates, and process error, which specifies the discrepancy between predicted and observed population sizes (Meyer and Millar 1999). Estimates of model parameters were calculated via Markov Chain Monte Carlo simulations using the WinBugs public-domain software. We specified uninformative or vague prior distributions for all model parameters. Once parameter estimates were available, we derived optimal harvest strategies with stochastic dynamic programming and simulated their use via the public-domain software ASDP (Lubow 1995). We assumed perfect control over harvest rates, but explicitly considered estimation error in key model parameters.

We examined a number of models in which K was either constant or allowed to vary over time. We present here only the results for the model with constant K. This model provides a reasonable fit to the data from both areas (Fig. 8) and suggests a similar K (Table 4). The intrinsic rate of growth r appears to be higher in California/Oregon and thus these mallards should be able to support slightly more harvest pressure over the long term than those originating from Alaska. However, we note there is a high degree of uncertainty associated with all parameter estimates.

Table 4. Estimates of carrying capacity K and the intrinsic rate of growth r from the logistic model for two groups of western mallards. (CI = Bayesian credibility intervals).

Stock	K	95% CI (K)	r	95% CI (r)
AK	0.95	0.68 – 1.09	0.36	0.14 – 0.64
CA/OR	0.88	0.60 – 1.09	0.46	0.20 – 0.94

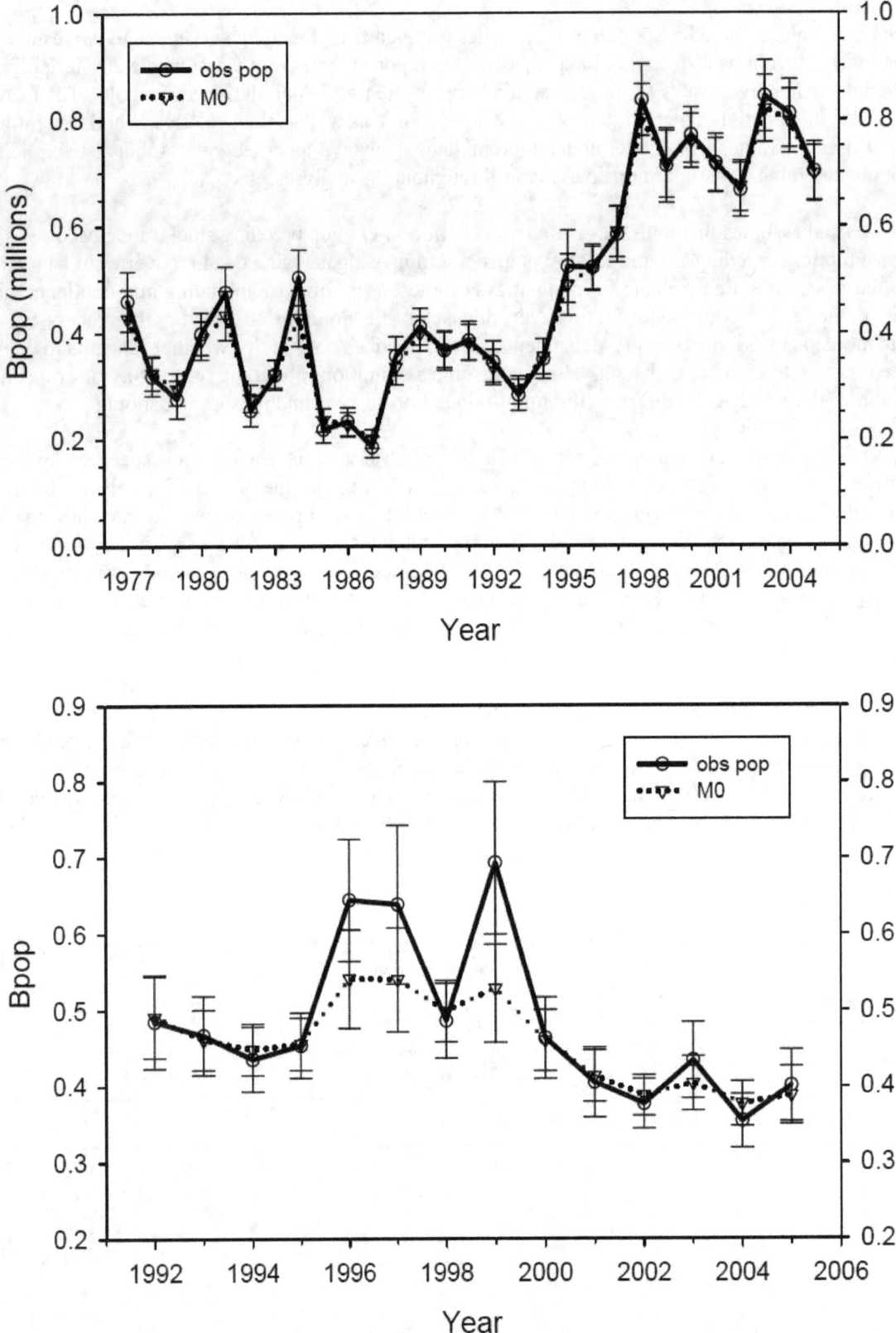

Fig. 8. Mallard breeding population size in Alaska (top) and California/Oregon (bottom) as estimated from surveys (obs pop) and those predicted from a logistic model that assumes a constant carrying capacity K (M0).

Harvest rates – We estimated harvest rates of adult male mallards in Alaska and California/Oregon directly from recoveries of reward bands placed on mallards prior to the hunting seasons in 2002-2005 (Table 5). Generally, these rates are similar to those for mid-continent mallards.

Table 5. Harvest rates (*h*, and standard errors, *se*) of adult-male mallards banded in Alaska and California/Oregon as based on reward banding. (There was an insufficient number of reward bandings in Alaska in 2005).

Year	AK		CA/OR	
	h	*se*	*h*	*se*
2002	0.1121	0.0306	0.1049	0.0109
2003	0.1000	0.0391	0.0970	0.0124
2004	0.0968	0.0379	0.1239	0.0175
2005			0.1086	0.0098
mean	0.1030	0.0057	0.1099	0.0082

Ultimately, the ability to predict stock-specific harvest rates as a function of flyway-specific regulations involves: (a) accounting for movements of breeding stocks to various harvest areas (flyways); (b) estimating harvest rates on mallards wintering in the various flyways; and (c) correlating these harvest rates with flyway framework regulations. This work is currently underway and may be completed prior to the 2007 regulations cycle.

HARVEST-MANAGEMENT OBJECTIVES

The basic harvest-management objective for mid-continent mallards is to maximize cumulative harvest over the long term, which inherently requires perpetuation of a viable population. Moreover, this objective is constrained to avoid regulations that could be expected to result in a subsequent population size below the goal of the North American Waterfowl Management Plan (NAWMP) (Fig. 9). According to this constraint, the value of harvest decreases proportionally as the difference between the goal and expected population size increases. This balance of harvest and population objectives results in a regulatory strategy that is more conservative than that for maximizing long-term harvest, but more liberal than a strategy to attain the NAWMP goal (regardless of effects on hunting opportunity). The current objective uses a population goal of 8.8 million mallards, which is based on 8.2 million mallards in the traditional survey area (from the 1998 update of the NAWMP) and a goal of 0.6 million for the combined states of Minnesota, Wisconsin, and Michigan.

For eastern mallards, there is no NAWMP goal or other established target for desired population size. Accordingly, the management objective for eastern mallards is simply to maximize long-term cumulative (i.e., sustainable) harvest.

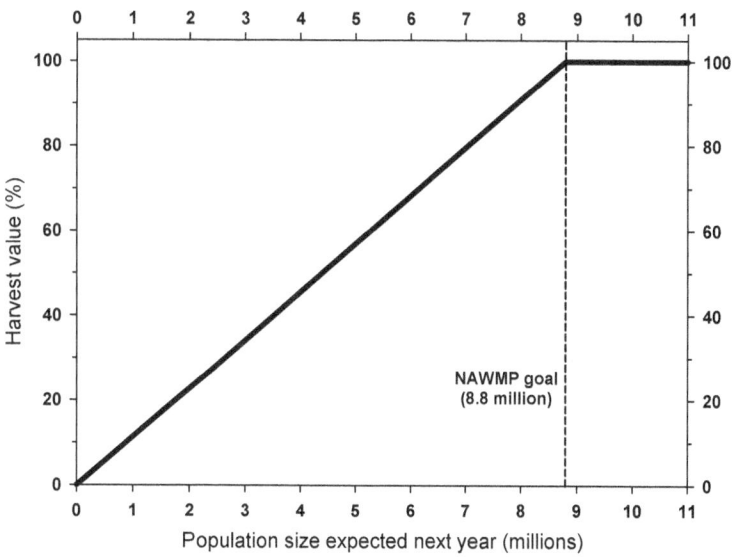

Fig. 9. The relative value of mid-continent mallard harvest, expressed as a function of breeding-population size expected in the subsequent year.

21

REGULATORY ALTERNATIVES

Evolution of Alternatives

When AHM was first implemented in 1995, three regulatory alternatives characterized as liberal, moderate, and restrictive were defined based on regulations used during 1979-84, 1985-87, and 1988-93, respectively. These regulatory alternatives also were considered for the 1996 hunting season. In 1997, the regulatory alternatives were modified to include: (1) the addition of a very-restrictive alternative; (2) additional days and a higher duck bag limit in the moderate and liberal alternatives; and (3) an increase in the bag limit of hen mallards in the moderate and liberal alternatives. In 2002 the USFWS further modified the moderate and liberal alternatives to include extensions of approximately one week in both the opening and closing framework dates.

In 2003 the very-restrictive alternative was eliminated at the request of the Flyway Councils. Expected harvest rates under the very-restrictive alternative did not differ significantly from those under the restrictive alternative, and the very-restrictive alternative was expected to be prescribed for <5% of all hunting seasons. Also, at the request of the Flyway Councils the USFWS agreed to exclude closed duck-hunting seasons from the AHM protocol when the breeding-population size of mid-continent mallards is >5.5 million (traditional survey area plus the Great Lakes region). Based on our assessment, closed hunting seasons do not appear to be necessary from the perspective of sustainable harvesting when the mid-continent mallard population exceeds this level. The impact of maintaining open seasons above this level also appears to be negligible for other mid-continent duck species (scaup, gadwall, wigeon, green-winged teal, blue-winged teal, shoveler, pintail, redhead, and canvasbacks), as based on population models developed by Johnson (2003). However, complete or partial season-closures for particular species or populations could still be deemed necessary in some situations regardless of the status of mid-continent mallards. Details of the regulatory alternatives for each Flyway are provided in Table 6.

Regulation-Specific Harvest Rates

Initially, harvest rates of mallards associated with each of the open-season regulatory alternatives were predicted using harvest-rate estimates from 1979-84, which were adjusted to reflect current hunter numbers and contemporary specifications of season lengths and bag limits. In the case of closed seasons in the U.S., we assumed rates of harvest would be similar to those observed in Canada during 1988-93, which was a period of restrictive regulations both in Canada and the U.S. All harvest-rate predictions were based only in part on band-recovery data, and relied heavily on models of hunting effort and success derived from hunter surveys (USFWS 2002: Appendix C). As such, these predictions had large sampling variances and their accuracy was uncertain.

In 2002 we began relying on Bayesian statistical methods for improving regulation-specific predictions of harvest rates, including predictions of the effects of framework-date extensions. Essentially, the idea is to use existing (prior) information to develop initial harvest-rate predictions (as above), to make regulatory decisions based on those predictions, and then to observe realized harvest rates. Those observed harvest rates, in turn, are treated as new sources of information for calculating updated (posterior) predictions. Bayesian methods are attractive because they provide a quantitative and formal, yet intuitive, approach to adaptive management.

Table 6. Regulatory alternatives for the 2006 duck-hunting season.

Regulation	Flyway			
	Atlantic[a]	Mississippi	Central[b]	Pacific[c]
Shooting hours	one-half hour before sunrise to sunset			
Framework dates				
Restrictive	Oct 1 - Jan 20	Saturday nearest Oct 1to the Sunday nearest Jan 20		
Moderate and Liberal	Saturday nearest September 24 to the last Sunday in January			
Season length (days)				
Restrictive	30	30	39	60
Moderate	45	45	60	86
Liberal	60	60	74	107
Bag limit (total / mallard / female mallard)				
Restrictive	3 / 3 / 1	3 / 2 / 1	3 / 3 / 1	4 / 3 / 1
Moderate	6 / 4 / 2	6 / 4 / 1	6 / 5 / 1	7 / 5 / 2
Liberal	6 / 4 / 2	6 / 4 / 2	6 / 5 / 2	7 / 7 / 2

[a] The states of Maine, Massachusetts, Connecticut, Pennsylvania, New Jersey, Maryland, Delaware, West Virginia, Virginia, and North Carolina are permitted to exclude Sundays, which are closed to hunting, from their total allotment of season days.
[b] The High Plains Mallard Management Unit is allowed 8, 12, and 23 extra days in the restrictive, moderate, and liberal alternatives, respectively.
[c] The Columbia Basin Mallard Management Unit is allowed seven extra days in the restrictive, and moderate alternatives.

For mid-continent mallards, we have empirical estimates of harvest rate from the recent period of liberal hunting regulations (1998-2005). The Bayesian methods thus allow us to combine these estimates with our prior predictions to provide updated estimates of harvest rates expected under the liberal regulatory alternative. Moreover, in the absence of experience (so far) with the restrictive and moderate regulatory alternatives, we reasoned that our initial predictions of harvest rates associated with those alternatives should be re-scaled based on a comparison of predicted and observed harvest rates under the liberal regulatory alternative. In other words, if observed harvest rates under the liberal alternative were 10% less than predicted, then we might also expect that the mean harvest rate under the moderate alternative would be 10% less than predicted. The appropriate scaling factors currently are based exclusively on prior beliefs about differences in mean harvest rate among regulatory alternatives, but they will be updated once we have experience with something other than the liberal alternative. A detailed description of the analytical framework for modeling mallard harvest rates is provided in Appendix B.

Our models of regulation-specific harvest rates also allow for the marginal effect of framework-date extensions in the moderate and liberal alternatives. A previous analysis by the USFWS (2001) suggested that implementation of framework-date extensions might be expected to increase the harvest rate of mid-continent mallards by about 15%, or in absolute terms by about 0.02 (SD = 0.01). Based on the observed harvest rate during the 2002-2005 hunting seasons, the updated (posterior) estimate of the marginal change in harvest rate attributable to the framework-date extension is 0.012 (SD = 0.008). Therefore, the estimated effect of the framework-date extension has been to increase harvest rate of mid-continent mallards by about 10% over what would otherwise be expected in the liberal alternative. However, the reader is strongly cautioned that reliable inference about the marginal effect of framework-date extensions ultimately depends on a rigorous experimental design (including controls and random application of treatments).

Current predictions of harvest rates of adult-male mid-continent mallards associated with each of the regulatory alternatives are provided in Table 7 and Fig. 9. Predictions of harvest rates for the other age-sex cohorts are based on the historical ratios of cohort-specific harvest rates to adult-male rates (Runge et al. 2002). These ratios are considered fixed at their long-term averages and are 1.5407, 0.7191, and 1.1175 for young males, adult females, and young females, respectively. We continued to make the simplifying assumption that the harvest rates of mid-continent mallards depend solely on the regulatory choice in the western three Flyways. This appears to be a reasonable assumption given the small proportion of mid-continent mallards wintering in the Atlantic Flyway (Munro and Kimball 1982), and harvest-rate predictions that suggest a minimal effect of Atlantic Flyway regulations (USFWS 2000). Under this assumption, the optimal regulatory strategy for the western three Flyways can be derived by ignoring the harvest regulations imposed in the Atlantic Flyway.

Table 7. Predictions of harvest rates of adult-male mid-continent mallards expected with application of the 2006 regulatory alternatives in the three western Flyways.

Regulatory alternative	Mean	SD
Closed (U.S.)	0.0088	0.0019
Restrictive	0.0583	0.0128
Moderate	0.1107	0.0216
Liberal	0.1269	0.0213

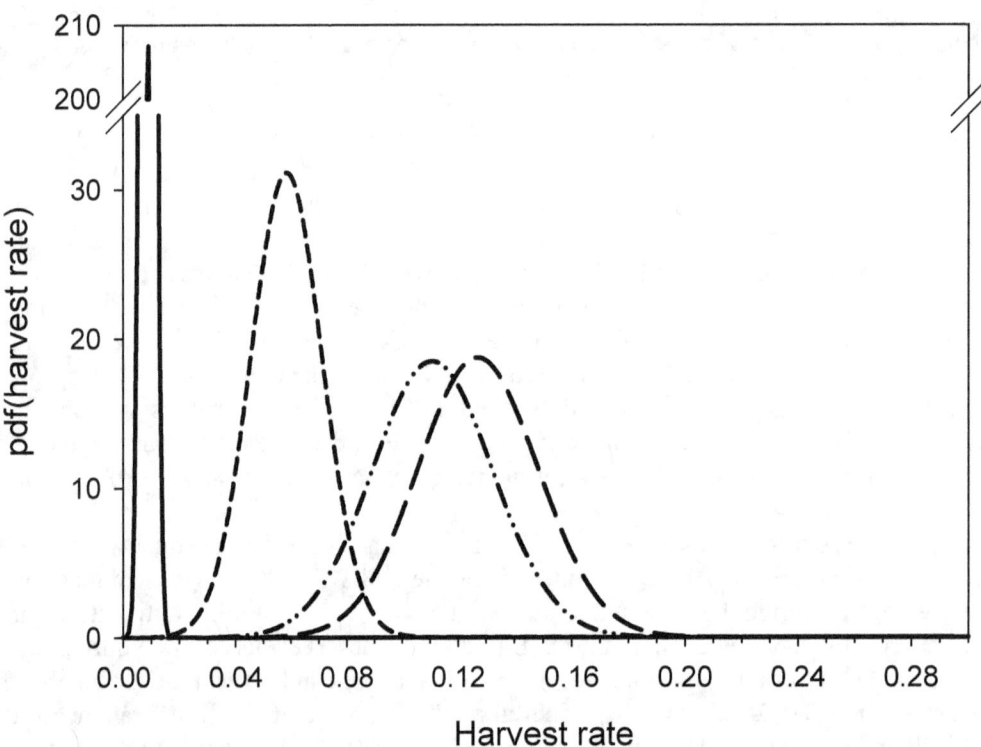

Fig. 9. Probability distributions of harvest rates of adult male mid-continent mallards expected with application of the 2006 regulatory alternatives in the three western Flyways.

Until last year, predictions of harvest rates for eastern mallards depended exclusively on historical (prior) information because more contemporary estimates of harvest rate were unavailable. However, we can now update the predictions of eastern-mallard harvest rates in the same fashion as that for mid-continent mallards based on reward banding conducted in eastern Canada and the northeastern U.S. (Appendix B). Like mid-continent mallards, harvest rates of age and sex cohorts other than adult male mallards are based on constant rates of differential vulnerability as derived from band-recovery data. For eastern mallards, these constants are 1.153, 1.331, and 1.509 for adult females, young males, and young females, respectively (Johnson et al. 2002a). Regulation-specific predictions of harvest rates of adult-male eastern mallards are provided in Table 8 and Fig. 10.

In contrast to mid-continent mallards, framework-date extensions were expected to increase the harvest rate of eastern mallards by only about 5% (USFWS 2001), or in absolute terms by about 0.01 (SD = 0.01). Based on the observed harvest rate during the 2002-2005 hunting seasons, the updated (posterior) estimate of the marginal change in harvest rate attributable to the framework-date extension is 0.006 (SD = 0.010). Therefore, the estimated effect of the framework-date extension has been to increase harvest rate of eastern mallards by about 4% over what would otherwise be expected in the liberal alternative.

Table 8. Predictions of harvest rates of adult-male eastern mallards expected with application of the 2006 regulatory alternatives in the Atlantic Flyway.

Regulatory alternative	Mean	SD
Closed (U.S.)	0.0797	0.0230
Restrictive	0.1209	0.0392
Moderate	0.1417	0.0473
Liberal	0.1636	0.0460

OPTIMAL REGULATORY STRATEGIES

We calculated optimal regulatory strategies using stochastic dynamic programming (Lubow 1995, Johnson and Williams 1999). For the three western Flyways, we based this optimization on: (1) the 2006 regulatory alternatives, including the closed-season constraint; (2) current population models and associated weights for mid-continent mallards; and (3) the dual objectives of maximizing long-term cumulative harvest and achieving a population goal of 8.8 million mid-continent mallards. The resulting regulatory strategy (Table 9) is similar to that used last year.

Assuming that regulatory choices adhered to this strategy (and that current model weights accurately reflect population dynamics), breeding-population size would be expected to average 7.37 million (SD = 1.77). Note that prescriptions for closed seasons in this strategy represent resource conditions that are insufficient to support one of the current regulatory alternatives, given current harvest-management objectives and constraints. However, closed seasons under all of these conditions are not necessarily required for long-term resource protection, and simply reflect the NAWMP population goal and the nature of the current regulatory alternatives.

Based on an observed population size of 7.86 million mid-continent mallards (traditional surveys plus MN, MI, and WI) and 4.45 million ponds in Prairie Canada, the optimal regulatory choice for the Pacific, Central, and Mississippi Flyways in 2006 is the liberal alternative.

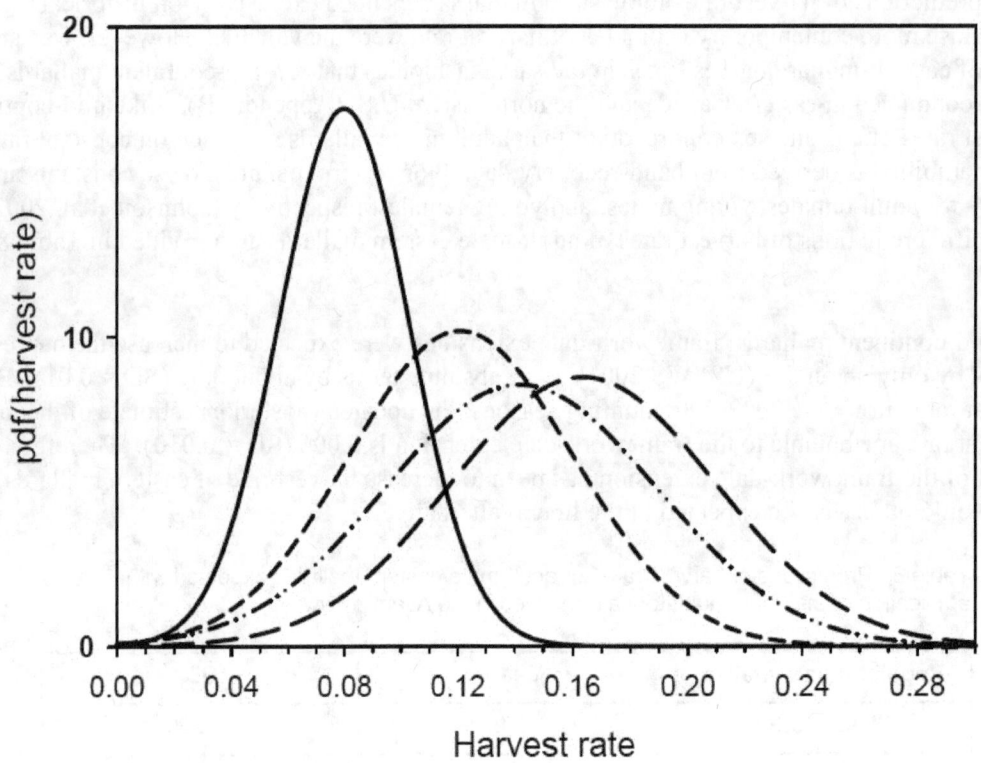

Fig. 10. Probability distributions of harvest rates of adult male eastern mallards expected with application of the 2005 regulatory alternatives in the Atlantic Flyway.

Table 9. Optimal regulatory strategy[a] for the three western Flyways for the 2006 hunting season. This strategy is based on current regulatory alternatives (including the closed-season constraint), on current mid-continent mallard models and weights, and on the dual objectives of maximizing long-term cumulative harvest and achieving a population goal of 8.8 million mallards. The shaded cell indicates the regulatory prescription for 2006.

Bpop[b]	Ponds[c]									
	1.5	2.0	2.5	3.0	3.5	4.0	4.5	5.0	5.5	6.0
≤5.25	C	C	C	C	C	C	C	C	C	C
5.50-6.25	R	R	R	R	R	R	R	R	R	R
6.50	R	R	R	R	R	R	R	R	M	M
6.75	R	R	R	R	R	R	R	M	M	L
7.00	R	R	R	R	M	M	M	L	L	L
7.25	R	R	R	M	M	L	L	L	L	L
7.50	R	R	M	M	L	L	L	L	L	L
7.75	M	L	L	L	L	L	L	L	L	L
8.00	M	L	L	L	L	L	L	L	L	L
≥8.25	L	L	L	L	L	L	L	L	L	L

[a] C = closed season, R = restrictive, M = moderate, L = liberal.
[b] Mallard breeding population size (in millions) in the traditional survey area (survey strata 1-18, 20-50, 75-77) and Michigan, Minnesota, and Wisconsin.
[c] Ponds (in millions) in Prairie Canada in May.

26

We calculated an optimal regulatory strategy for the Atlantic Flyway based on: (1) the 2006 regulatory alternatives; (2) current population models and associated weights for eastern mallards; and (3) an objective to maximize long-term cumulative harvest. The resulting strategy suggests liberal regulations for all population sizes of record, and is characterized by a lack of intermediate regulations (Table 10). The strategy exhibits this behavior in part because of the small differences in harvest rate among regulatory alternatives (Fig. 10).

Table 10. Optimal regulatory strategy[a] for the Atlantic Flyway for the 2006 hunting season. This strategy is based on current regulatory alternatives, on current eastern mallard models and weights, and on an objective to maximize long-term cumulative harvest. The shaded cell indicates the regulatory prescription for 2006.

Mallards[b]	Regulation
<225	C
225	R
>225	L

[a] C = closed season, R = restrictive, M = moderate, and L = liberal.
[b] Estimated number of mallards in eastern Canada (survey strata 51-54, 56) and the northeastern U.S. (state plot surveys), in thousands.

We simulated the use of the regulatory strategy in Table 10 to determine expected performance characteristics. Assuming that harvest management adhered to this strategy (and that current model weights accurately reflect population dynamics), the annual breeding-population size would be expected to average 872 thousand (SD = 16 thousand). Based on a breeding population size of 899 thousand mallards, the optimal regulatory choice for the Atlantic Flyway in 2006 is the liberal alternative.

Application of AHM Concepts to Species of Concern

The USFWS is striving to apply the principles and tools of AHM to improve decision-making for several species of special concern. We here report on four such efforts in which progress has been made since last year. This work is being conducted as a joint effort with USGS and we particularly appreciate the technical assistance provided M. C. Runge (Patuxent Wildlife Research Center) and M. J. Conroy (Georgia Cooperative Fish and Wildlife Research Unit).

Pintails

Pursuant to requests from the Service Regulations Committee and the Pacific Flyway Council, we reviewed available information about northern pintail (*Anas acuta*) demography, population dynamics, and harvest (http://www.fws.gov/migratorybirds/reports/ahm05/NOPI%202005%20Report%202.pdf). Based on this review, several technical improvements in our ability to model pintail harvest dynamics have been adopted. In addition, we undertook an effort to evaluate pintail harvest potential based on these model improvements and to explore the impacts of these improvements on past and future pintail harvest management policy.

Breeding population survey corrections.--There is general agreement among waterfowl biologists that the May breeding population survey undercounts pintails in dry years when pintails tend to settle farther north on the breeding grounds. We developed a method to correct the observed breeding population estimates for this bias. The effect of this correction is to remove some of the apparent sharp drops in pintail numbers during dry years. Further, this correction suggests that in recent years, there were 30-60% more pintails in the breeding population

27

than the May surveys indicated.

Updated recruitment, harvest, and population Models.--We developed improved methods to predict recruitment and harvest, and included these components in an updated population model for use in the pintail harvest strategy. The recruitment model uses latitude of the pintail population and the corrected breeding population size estimates as predictors. The harvest models identify a "season-within-a-season" effect in the Central and Mississippi flyways. The new population model predicts population change better than the previous model.

Pintail harvest potential.--Using the new pintail population model, we were able to analyze the harvest potential of the pintail population. There is evidence that the pintail population is settling, on average, about 2.4° of latitude farther north now than it did prior to 1975, possibly as a result of large-scale changes in habitat. This more northern distribution has resulted in lower reproduction, a 30-45% decrease in carrying capacity, and a 40-65% decrease in sustainable harvest potential.

Incorporating the technical improvements described above into the population model, we can calculate and depict the current harvest strategy (Fig. 11). The season would be closed when the *observed* BPOP is less than ~1 million (which is roughly equivalent to a corrected fall flight of 2 million), restrictive when the observed BPOP is less than 2.5 million with a high latitude of the BPOP, and liberal otherwise (this graph assumes the AHM package is liberal; the restrictive section of the graph implies a season-within-a-season). More than one bird in the bag is allowed when the population growth is expected to be greater than 6%. The corresponding state-dependent harvest policies when the AHM package is moderate or restrictive are shown in Fig. 12. When the AHM package is moderate, a restrictive season-within-a-season is possible. When the AHM package is restrictive, the pintail season is either also restrictive, or else closed.

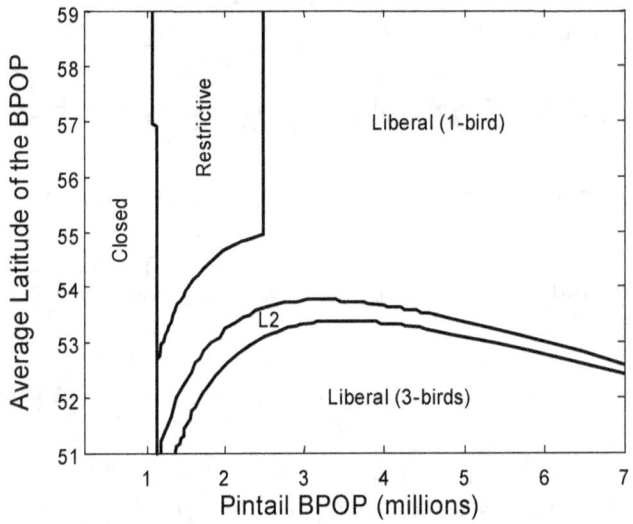

Fig. 11. Pintail harvest strategy for a liberal duck season, based on the overflight bias correction, new recruitment model, and updated harvest models. For a given value of the *observed* (not corrected) pintail BPOP and average latitude of the BPOP, the resulting regulatory decision is shown. Note that this graph assumes the AHM package is "liberal", thus the "restrictive" regulation implies a season-within-a-season.

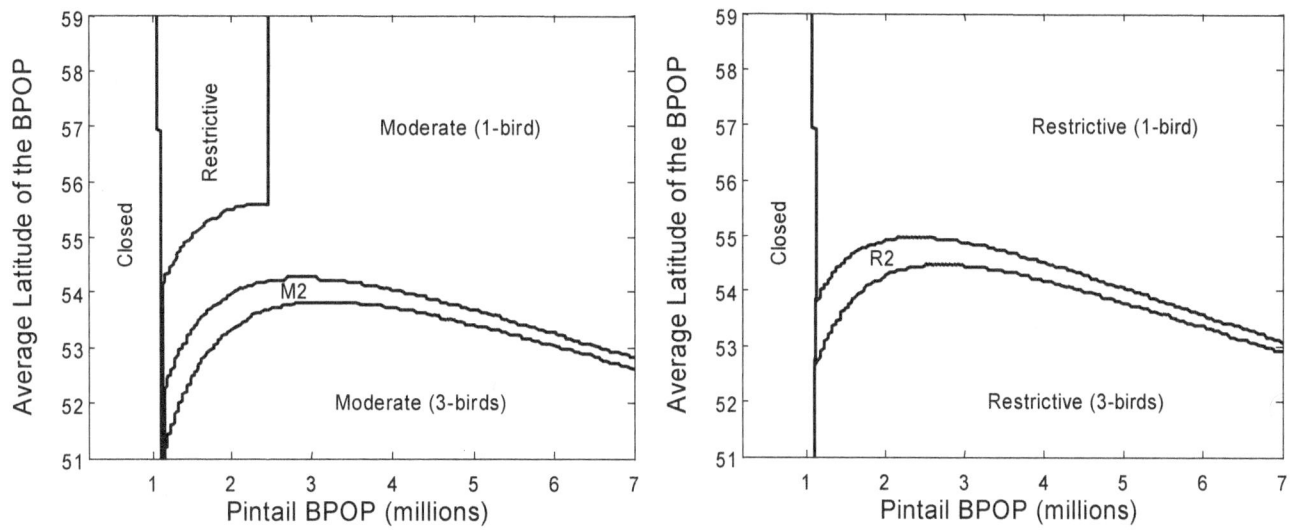

Fig. 12. State-dependent pintail harvest strategy, given a moderate AHM alternative (left) and a restrictive AHM alternative (right). For details see Fig. 11.

Black Ducks

We continued to examine the harvest potential of black ducks using models of population dynamics described by Conroy et al. (2002). These models incorporate the most controversial hypotheses about reproductive and survival processes in black ducks, and also allow for the possibility that extant estimates of reproductive and survival rates are positively biased. Using empirically based model weights (from 1962-93) in conjunction with deterministic dynamic programming, we can derive combinations of equilibrium population size and harvest for a range of adult harvest rates. Because of evidence that the reproductive rate of black ducks declines with increasing numbers of mallards, the carrying capacity and harvestable surplus of black ducks are smaller with higher numbers of sympatric mallards.

There also appears be a temporal decline in the reproductive rate of black ducks that cannot be explained by changes in black duck and mallard abundance. The cause is unknown but may be related to declines in the quantity and/or quality of breeding habitat, wintering habitat, or both. Whatever the cause, the management implications are profound, suggesting that carrying capacity and maximum sustainable harvest of black ducks have decreased by 35% and 60%, respectively, in the past two decades (Fig. 13).

Since 1983, the U.S. Fish and Wildlife Service has been operating under guidance provided in an Environmental Assessment that specified states harvesting significant numbers of black ducks achieve at least a 25% reduction in harvest from 1977- 81 levels. Although this level of harvest reduction has been achieved, black duck harvest rates appear to have increased with the return of 50-60 day duck hunting seasons associated with implementation of AHM (Fig. 14). Whether these harvest rates are appropriate given current population status is unclear; based on black duck counts in the midwinter survey, current rates might be at or above maximum sustainable levels. However, a recent publication by Link et al. (2006), which compared the U.S. midwinter survey with the Christmas Bird Count, suggests that a larger portion of the black duck population may now be wintering in Canada than in the past. If this is the case, then regulatory prescriptions based on the U.S. midwinter survey could be overly conservative. Therefore, the USFWS, USGS, the Atlantic and Mississippi Flyways, and CWS are aggressively pursuing efforts to develop an adaptive framework based on breeding-population surveys and internationally agreed-upon management objectives.

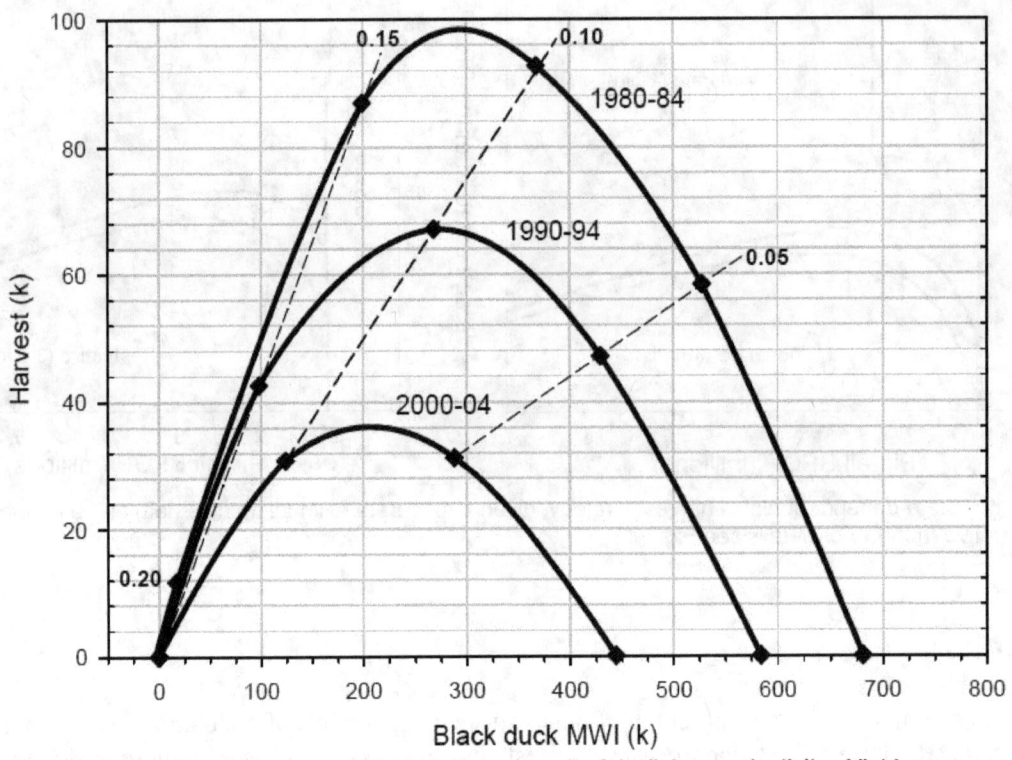

Fig 13. Collapsing yield curves of black ducks as result of declining productivity. Yield curves were based on population models provided by Conroy et al. (2002). For each period, we used the median year to represent black duck productivity and fixed the number of mallards at their average midwinter count. The diagonal lines intersect the indicated adult harvest rate on each yield curve.

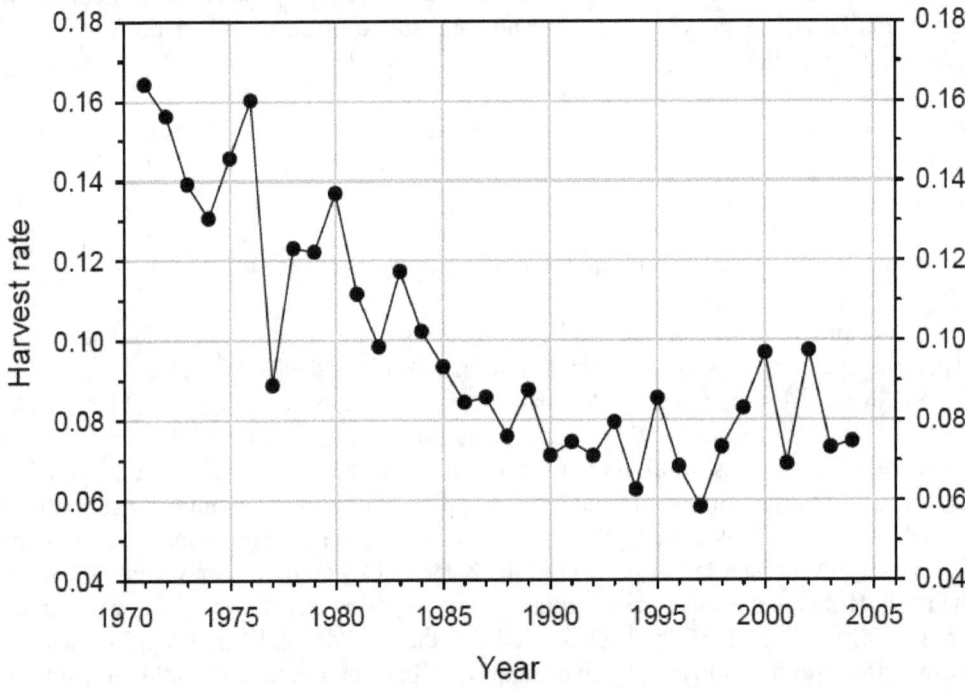

Fig 14. Estimates of harvest rates of adult-male black ducks based on recoveries of standard bands, adjusted for preliminary estimates of band-reporting rates (P. Garrettson, unpubl. data).

Scaup

We continued to evaluate the harvest potential of the continental scaup (greater *Aythya marila* and lesser *Aythya affinis*) population using a discrete, logistic population model and available monitoring information on scaup population and harvest dynamics (http://www.fws.gov/migratorybirds/reports/ahm05/scaupharvestpotential.pdf). We used a fully Bayesian approach to estimate scaup population parameters and to characterize the uncertainty related to scaup harvest potential (Table 11.).

We plotted mean scaup equilibrium population sizes and corresponding sustainable harvests (Fig. 15) along with 95% credibility intervals (gray shading). This yield curve, in combination with observed harvests and breeding population sizes from 1994 – 2005, suggests that current harvests may be at maximum sustainable levels.

Table 11. Estimates of model and management parameters (posterior means and 95% credibility intervals) derived from fitting a logistic population model to continental scaup populations using a Bayesian hierarchical approach. (r = intrinsic rate of growth, K = carrying capacity, MSY = maximum sustainable yield, h_{MSY} = harvest rate at MSY, and $BPOP_{MSY}$ = breeding population size at MSY)

Parameter	mean	2.50%	97.50%
r	0.1763	0.0978	0.2974
K	8.6259	6.4830	11.450
MSY	0.3694	0.2271	0.5377
h_{MSY}	0.0881	0.0489	0.1487
$BPOP_{MSY}$	4.3129	3.2420	5.7230

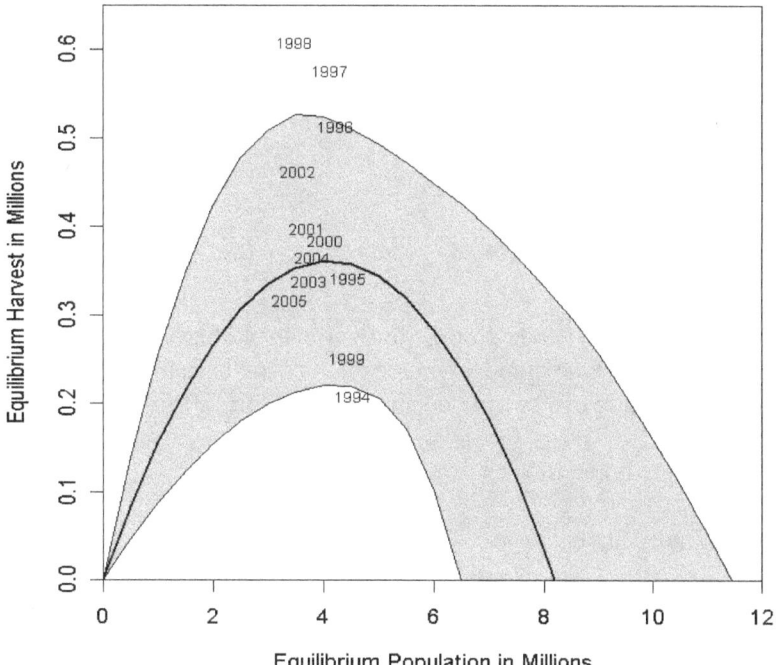

Fig. 15. Equilibrium population sizes and harvests (shaded area represents 95% credibility interval) estimated for continental scaup populations from a logistic model using a Bayesian hierarchical approach. The years represent recent combinations of observed population size and harvest.

31

Atlantic Population of Canada Geese

For the purposes of this AHM application, Atlantic Population Canada Geese (APCG) are defined as those geese breeding on the Ungava Peninsula. By this delineation, we assume that geese in the Atlantic population outside this area are either few in number, similar in population dynamics to the Ungava birds, or both.

To account for heterogeneity among individuals, we developed a base model consisting of a truncated time-invariant age-based projection model to describe the dynamics of APCG,

$$\mathbf{n}(t+1)=\mathbf{A}\mathbf{n}(t),$$

where $\mathbf{n}(t)$ is a vector of the abundances of the ages in the population at time t, and $\mathbf{A}$ is the population projection matrix, whose ijth entry a_{ij} gives the contribution of an individual in stage j to stage i over 1 time step. The projection interval (from t to $t+1$) is one year, with the census being taken in mid-June (i.e., this model has a pre-breeding census). The life cycle diagram reflecting the transition sequence is:

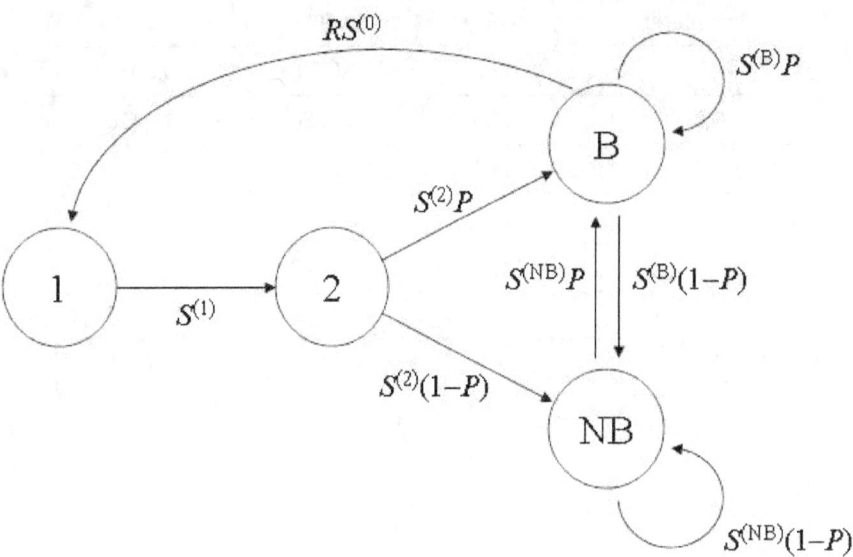

where node 1 refers to one-year-old birds, node 2 refers to two-year-old birds, node B refers to adult breeders, and node NB refers to adult non-breeders. One immediate extension of the base model is to remove the assumption of time-invariance, and express the parameters as time-dependent quantities:

P_t = proportion of adult birds in population in year t which breed;

R_t = basic breeding productivity in year t (per capita);

$S_t^{(0)}$ = annual survival rate of young from fledging in year t to the census point the next year;

$S_t^{(1)}$ = annual survival rate of one-year-old birds in year t; etc.

For APCG, only $N^{(B)}$, R and z are observable annually, where $N^{(B)}$ is the number of breeding adults, R is the per capita reproductive rate (ratio of fledged young to breeding adults), and z is an extrinsic variable (a function of timing of snow melt on the breeding grounds).

Note that at the time of the management decision in the United States (July), estimates for only the breeding population size and the environmental variable(s) are available; the age-ratio isn't estimated until later in the summer. Thus, in year t, the observable state variables are $N_t^{(B)}$, z_t, and R_{t-1}.

There are several other state variables of interest, however, namely, $N^{(1)}$, $N^{(2)}$, and $N^{(NB)}$. Because annual harvest decisions need to be made based on the total population size (N^{tot}), which is the sum of contributions from various non-breeding age classes as well as the number of breeding individuals, abundance of non-breeding individuals ($N^{(NB)}$, $N^{(1)}$, and $N^{(2)}$) needs to be derived using population-reconstruction techniques. In most cases, population reconstruction involves estimating the most likely population projection matrix, given a time series of population vectors (where number of individuals in each age class at each time is known). However, in our case, only estimates of N^B, R and z are available (not the complete population vector); in effect, we must estimate some of the population abundance values given the other parameters in the model. Recent extensions of Bayesian statistical methods to population reconstruction may provide an adequate solution (Fig. 16).

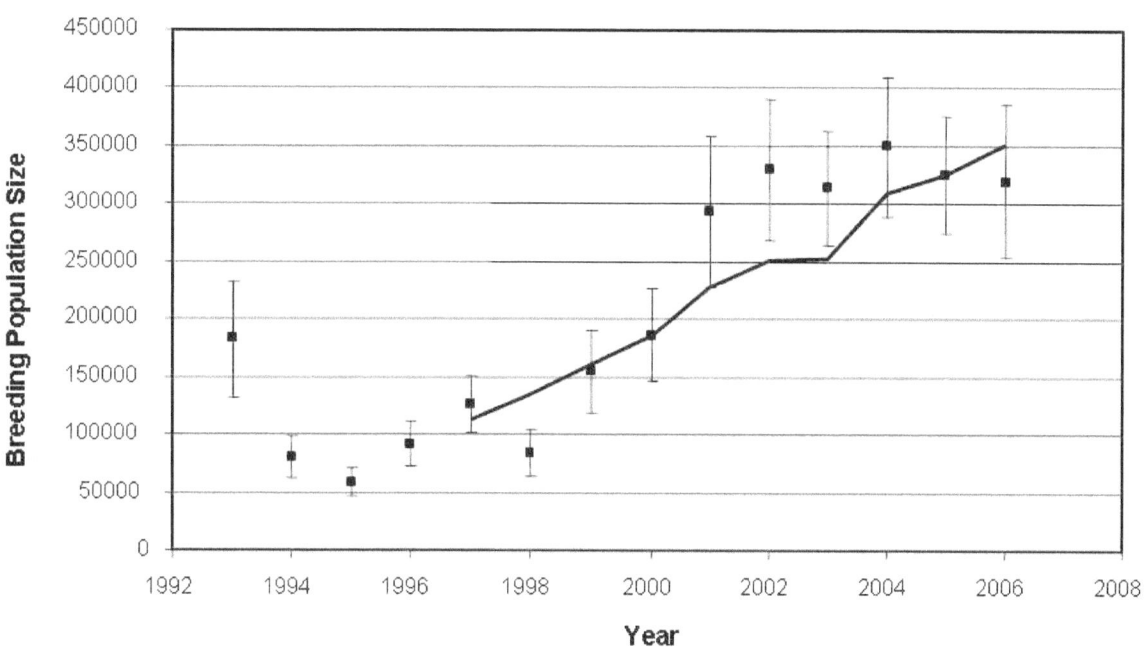

Fig.16. Observed breeding population size of Atlantic Population Canada Geese (estimates and 95% confidence bounds) compared with the population trajectory based on our population model and population reconstruction techniques

Management of the APCG has, in recent years, been focused on achieving the minimum population needed to sustain some level of sport harvest. However, there is growing concern over the potential problems caused by overabundant goose species, and management objectives for goose species are increasingly considering population control as an important objective.

Specification of an explicit, mathematical objective function for APCG will require careful deliberation among the appropriate stakeholders. Since formal AHM is an exercise in optimization, the objective often not only drives the outcome, but also strongly influences the development of the other components of the decision framework (e.g., the decision variables, the projection model, etc.). As a starting point for our work in developing an AHM application for APCG, and as a starting point for discussions about the management objectives for this resource, we developed a candidate objective function. We propose that the management objective needs to reflect the simultaneous problem of maximizing opportunity for harvest, while minimizing the risk that the population will become either too large (i.e., beyond human tolerance in terms of impacts on habitat or other species), or too small (i.e., requiring season closure for political reasons).

We believe that the critical components governing the dynamics of APCG, unlike those governing ducks, are generally density-independent over the range of population sizes that likely characterize management objectives; as such, harvest represents an imposed regulatory mechanism on the dynamics of the population. This requires specification of a desired range for the population size. Let N^{MTP} represent the <u>m</u>aximum <u>t</u>olerable <u>p</u>opulation size that stakeholders would accept, given the potential for negative impacts of overabundant APCG on stakeholder interests. Let N^{Min} be the <u>min</u>imum tolerable population size, below which season closure is the only politically viable management option. The management objective is to maintain the population in the range between the maximum and minimum values, while simultaneously maximizing opportunity for sport harvest.

There is another implicit dynamic that may interact with this objective: there may be a limit to the amount of harvest that could be induced with traditional harvest regulations. Let N^{MCP} represent the <u>m</u>aximum <u>c</u>ontrollable <u>p</u>opulation level that could be regulated by harvest (a function of a finite number of goose hunters or hunting effort; this is currently an unknown quantity for APCG). We think it's most likely that $N^{\text{MTP}} < N^{\text{MCP}}$, although this assumption won't affect the development of any other aspect of the AHM protocol. N^{MCP} might strongly affect the optimal policy, however, as the policy should avoid letting the population reach an uncontrollable level, especially if that level is also intolerable. Thus, the objective should implicitly minimize the risk of losing the ability to control the population. Note that N^{MCP} should be calculated from biological considerations in conjunction with information about the limits to harvest. N^{MTP}, however, is a purely sociological constraint.

We think this objective will hold the population as close to the maximum tolerable population size as possible (thus, allowing the greatest harvest), while guarding against the risk of the population getting out of control.

Mathematically, these objectives can be expressed as

$$\max \sum_{t=0}^{\infty} u(N_t) H_t,$$

that is, maximizing the long-term cumulative harvest utility, where the value (utility) of harvest is decremented relative to the bounds of the constraint (i.e., the maximum and minimum bounds). One possible form of the utility function u is a 'square-wave', where utility of the harvest is 0 when the population size is above and below N^{MTP} and N^{Min}, respectively. The Atlantic Flyway Canada Goose Committee (AFCGC) has proposed values for N^{MTP} and N^{Min} (Fig. 17).

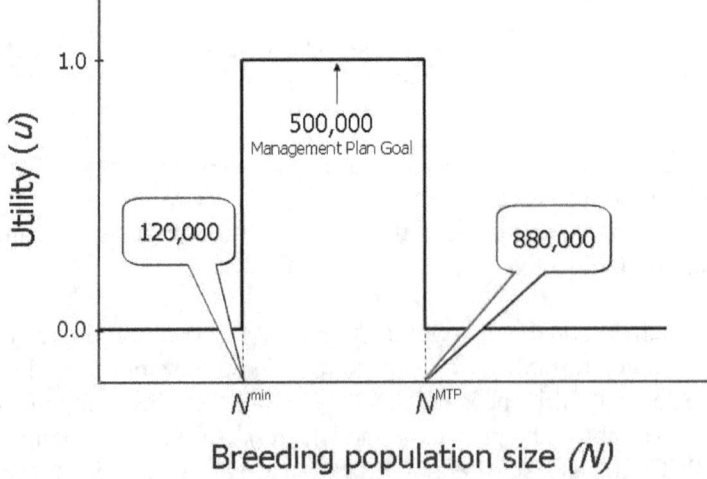

Fig. 17. Proposed utility of APCG harvest as a function of breeding-population size.

34

The AFCGC would also like to consider a management objective to avoid overly restrictive regulations when populations are close to goal, as well as abrupt changes in regulations with relatively small changes in population size or spring weather conditions (i.e., a "knife-edged" strategy). One way this may be accomplished is by adding a cost that increases with increasing harvest rates to the objective function. The addition of this cost is sufficient to induce more intermediate harvest rates in the optimal harvest strategy (Fig. 18).

Development of a preliminary AHM framework for APCG is nearing completion and, pending sufficient review and evaluation, may be ready for implementation in 2007.

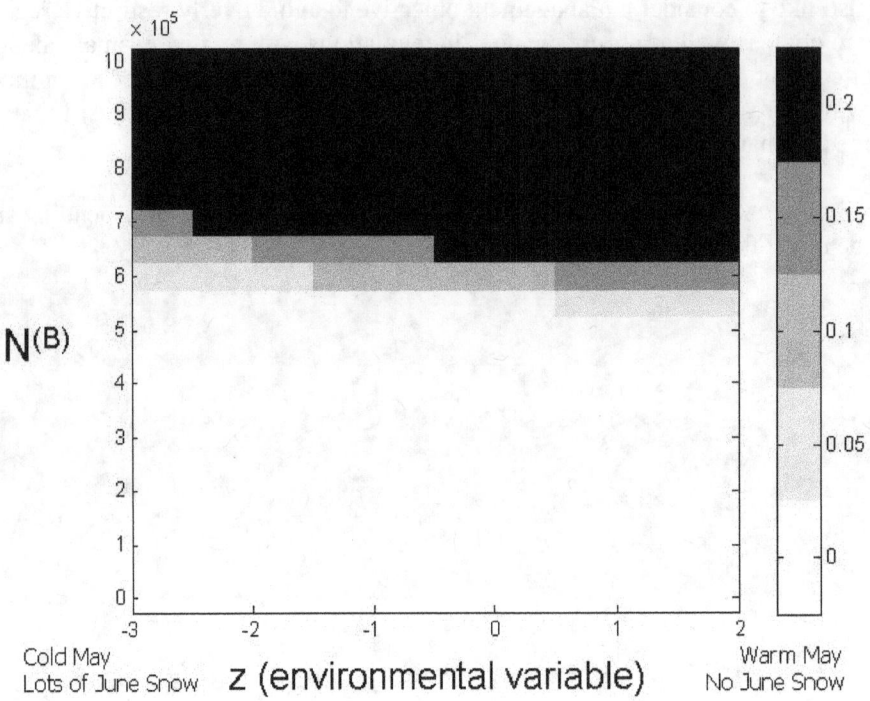

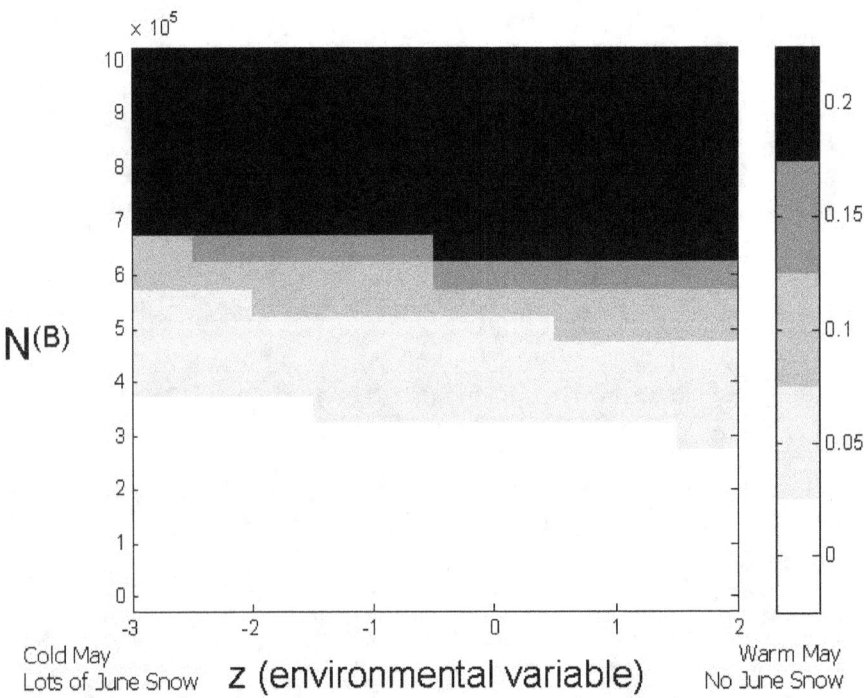

Fig. 18. Optimal harvest rates for APCG at a stable stage distribution where there is no cost (above) and a relatively high cost (below) for a knife-edged harvest strategy.

LITERATURE CITED

Anderson, D. R., and K. P. Burnham. 1976. Population ecology of the mallard. VI. The effect of exploitation on survival. U.S. Fish and Wildlife Service Resource Publication No. 128. 66pp.

Blohm, R. J. 1989. Introduction to harvest - understanding surveys and season setting. Proceedings of the International Waterfowl Symposium 6:118-133.

Blohm, R. J., R. E. Reynolds, J. P. Bladen, J. D. Nichols, J. E. Hines, K. P. Pollock, and R. T. Eberhardt. 1987. Mallard mortality rates on key breeding and wintering areas. Transactions of the North American Wildlife and Natural Resources Conference 52:246-263.

Burnham, K. P., G. C. White, and D. R. Anderson. 1984. Estimating the effect of hunting on annual survival rates of adult mallards. Journal of Wildlife Management 48:350-361.

Conroy, M. J., M. W. Miller, and J. E. Hines. 2002. Identification and synthetic modeling of factors affecting American black duck populations. Wildlife Monographs 150. 64pp.

Heusman, H W, and J. R. Sauer. 2000. The northeastern states' waterfowl breeding population survey. Wildlife Society Bulletin 28:355-364.

Johnson, F. A. 2003. Population dynamics of ducks other than mallards in mid-continent North America. Draft. Fish and Wildlife Service, U.S. Dept. Interior, Washington, D.C. 15pp.

Johnson, F. A., J. A. Dubovsky, M. C. Runge, and D. R. Eggeman. 2002*a*. A revised protocol for the adaptive harvest management of eastern mallards. Fish and Wildlife Service, U.S. Dept. Interior, Washington, D.C. 13pp. [online] URL: http://migratorybirds.fws.gov/reports/ahm02/emal-ahm-2002.pdf.

Johnson, F. A., W. L. Kendall, and J. A. Dubovsky. 2002*b*. Conditions and limitations on learning in the adaptive management of mallard harvests. Wildlife Society Bulletin 30:176-185.

Johnson, F. A., C. T. Moore, W. L. Kendall, J. A. Dubovsky, D. F. Caithamer, J. R. Kelley, Jr., and B. K. Williams. 1997. Uncertainty and the management of mallard harvests. Journal of Wildlife Management 61:202-216.

Johnson, F. A., and B. K. Williams. 1999. Protocol and practice in the adaptive management of waterfowl harvests. Conservation Ecology 3(1): 8. [online] URL: http://www.consecol.org/vol3/iss1/art8.

Johnson, F. A., B. K. Williams, J. D. Nichols, J. E. Hines, W. L. Kendall, G. W. Smith, and D. F. Caithamer. 1993. Developing an adaptive management strategy for harvesting waterfowl in North America. Transactions of the North American Wildlife and Natural Resources Conference 58:565-583.

Johnson, F. A., B. K. Williams, and P. R. Schmidt. 1996. Adaptive decision-making in waterfowl harvest and habitat management. Proceedings of the International Waterfowl Symposium 7:26-33.

Link, W. A., J. R. Sauer, and D. K. Niven. 2006. A hierarchical model for regional analysis of population change using Christmas bird count data, with application to the American black duck. The Condor 108:13-24.

Lubow, B. C. 1995. SDP: Generalized software for solving stochastic dynamic optimization problems. Wildlife Society Bulletin 23:738-742.

Meyer, R., and R. B. Millar. 1999. BUGS in Bayesian stock assessments. Canadian Journal of Fisheries and Aquatic Sciences 56:1078-1086.

Munro, R. E., and C. F. Kimball. 1982. Population ecology of the mallard. VII. Distribution and derivation of the harvest. U.S. Fish and Wildlife Service Resource Publication 147. 127pp.

Nichols, J. D., F. A. Johnson, and B. K. Williams. 1995. Managing North American waterfowl in the face of uncertainty. Annual Review of Ecology and Systematics 26:177-199.

Runge, M. C., F. A. Johnson, J. A. Dubovsky, W. L. Kendall, J. Lawrence, and J. Gammonley. 2002. A revised protocol for the adaptive harvest management of mid-continent mallards. Fish and Wildlife Service, U.S. Dept. Interior, Washington, D.C. 28pp. [online] URL: http://migratorybirds.fws.gov/reports/ahm02/MCMrevise2002.pdf.

U.S. Fish and Wildlife Service. 2000. Adaptive harvest management: 2000 duck hunting season. U.S. Dept. Interior, Washington. D.C. 43pp. [online] URL: http://migratorybirds.fws.gov/reports/ahm00/ahm2000.pdf.

U.S. Fish and Wildlife Service. 2001. Framework-date extensions for duck hunting in the United States: projected impacts & coping with uncertainty, U.S. Dept. Interior, Washington, D.C. 8pp. [online] URL: http://migratorybirds.fws.gov/reports/ahm01/fwassess.pdf.

U.S. Fish and Wildlife Service. 2002. Adaptive harvest management: 2002 duck hunting season. U.S. Dept. Interior, Washington. D.C. 34pp. [online] URL: http://migratorybirds.fws.gov/reports/ahm02/2002-AHM-report.pdf.

Walters, C. J. 1986. Adaptive management of renewable resources. MacMillan Publ. Co., New York, N.Y. 374pp.

Williams, B. K., and F. A. Johnson. 1995. Adaptive management and the regulation of waterfowl harvests. Wildlife Society Bulletin 23:430-436.

Williams, B. K., F. A. Johnson, and K. Wilkins. 1996. Uncertainty and the adaptive management of waterfowl harvests. Journal of Wildlife Management 60:223-232.

APPENDIX A: AHM Working Group

(Note: This list includes only permanent members of the AHM Working Group. Not listed here are numerous persons from federal and state agencies that assist the Working Group on an ad-hoc basis.)

Coordinator:

Fred Johnson
U.S. Fish & Wildlife Service
McCarty C 420, University of Florida
P.O. Box 110339
Gainesville, FL 32611
phone: 352-392-3052
fax: 352-392-8555
e-mail: fred_a_johnson@fws.gov

USFWS representatives:

Bob Blohm (Region 9)
U.S. Fish and Wildlife Service
4401 N Fairfax Drive
MS MSP-4107
Arlington, VA 22203
phone: 703-358-1966
fax: 703-358-2272
e-mail: robert_blohm@fws.gov

Brad Bortner (Region 1)
U.S. Fish and Wildlife Service
911 NE 11th Ave.
Portland, OR 97232-4181
phone: 503-231-6164
fax: 503-231-2364
e-mail: brad_bortner@fws.gov

David Viker (Region 4)
U.S. Fish and Wildlife Service
1875 Century Blvd., Suite 345
Atlanta, GA 30345
phone: 404-679-7188
fax: 404-679-7285
e-mail: david_viker@fws.gov

Dave Case (contractor)
D.J. Case & Associates
607 Lincolnway West
Mishawaka, IN 46544
phone: 574-258-0100
fax: 574-258-0189
e-mail: dave@djcase.com

John Cornely (Region 6)
U.S. Fish and Wildlife Service
P.O. Box 25486, DFC
Denver, CO 80225
phone: 303-236-8155 (ext 259)
fax: 303-236-8680
e-mail: john_cornely@fws.gov

Ken Gamble (Region 9)
U.S. Fish and Wildlife Service
101 Park DeVille Drive, Suite B
Columbia, MO 65203
phone: 573-234-1473
fax: 573-234-1475
e-mail: ken_gamble@fws.gov

Diane Pence (Region 5)
U.S. Fish and Wildlife Service
300 Westgate Center Drive
Hadley, MA 01035-9589
phone: 413-253-8577
fax: 413-253-8424
e-mail: diane_pence@fws.gov

Jeff Haskins (Region 2)
U.S. Fish and Wildlife Service
P.O. Box 1306
Albuquerque, NM 87103
phone: 505-248-6827 (ext 30)
fax: 505-248-7885
e-mail: jeff_haskins@fws.gov

Bob Leedy (Region 7)
U.S. Fish and Wildlife Service
1011 East Tudor Road
Anchorage, AK 99503-6119
phone: 907-786-3446
fax: 907-786-3641
e-mail: robert_leedy@fws.gov

Jerry Serie (Region 9)
U.S. Fish and Wildlife Service
11510 American Holly Drive
Laurel, MD 20708
phone: 301-497-5851
fax: 301-497-5885
e-mail: jerry_serie@fws.gov

Dave Sharp (Region 9)
U.S. Fish and Wildlife Service
P.O. Box 25486, DFC
Denver, CO 80225-0486
phone: 303-275-2386
fax: 303-275-2384
e-mail: dave_sharp@fws.gov

Bob Trost (Region 9)
U.S. Fish and Wildlife Service
911 NE 11th Ave.
Portland, OR 97232-4181
phone: 503-231-6162
fax: 503-231-6228
e-mail: robert_trost@fws.gov

Sean Kelly (Region 3)
U.S. Fish and Wildlife Service
1 Federal Drive
Ft. Snelling, MN 55111-4056
phone: 612-713-5470
fax: 612-713-5393
e-mail: sean_kelly@fws.gov

Canadian Wildlife Service representatives:

Dale Caswell
Canadian Wildlife Service
123 Main St. Suite 150
Winnepeg, Manitoba, Canada R3C 4W2
phone: 204-983-5260
fax: 204-983-5248
e-mail: dale.caswell@ec.gc.ca

Eric Reed
Canadian Wildlife Service
351 St. Joseph Boulevard
Hull, QC K1A OH3, Canada
phone: 819-953-0294
fax: 819-953-6283
e-mail: eric.reed@ec.gc.ca

Flyway Council representatives:

Scott Baker (Mississippi Flyway)
Mississippi Dept. of Wildlife, Fisheries, and Parks
P.O. Box 378
Redwood, MS 39156
 phone: 601-661-0294
fax: 601-364-2209
e-mail: mahannah1@aol.com

Diane Eggeman (Atlantic Flyway)
Florida Fish and Wildlife Conservation Commission
8932 Apalachee Pkwy.
Tallahassee, FL 32311
phone: 850-488-5878
fax: 850-488-5884
e-mail: diane.eggeman@fwc.state.fl.us

Jim Gammonley (Central Flyway)
Colorado Division of Wildlife
317 West Prospect
Fort Collins, CO 80526
phone: 970-472-4379
fax: 970-472-4457
e-mail: jim.gammonley@state.co.us

Mike Johnson (Central Flyway)
North Dakota Game and Fish Department
100 North Bismarck Expressway
Bismarck, ND 58501-5095
phone: 701-328-6319
fax: 701-328-6352
e-mail: mjohnson@state.nd.us

Don Kraege (Pacific Flyway)
Washington Dept. of Fish and Wildlife
600 Capital Way North
Olympia. WA 98501-1091
phone: 360-902-2509
fax: 360-902-2162
e-mail: kraegdkk@dfw.wa.gov

Bryan Swift (Atlantic Flyway)
Dept. Environmental Conservation
625 Broadway
Albany, NY 12233-4754
phone: 518-402-8866
fax: 518-402-9027 or 402-8925
e-mail: blswift@gw.dec.state.ny.us

Dan Yparraguirre (Pacific Flyway)
California Dept. of Fish and Game
1812 Ninth Street
Sacramento, CA 95814
phone: 916-445-3685
e-mail: dyparraguirre@dfg.ca.gov

Guy Zenner (Mississippi Flyway)
Iowa Dept. of Natural Resources
1203 North Shore Drive
Clear Lake, IA   50428
phone: 515/357-3517, ext. 23
fax: 515-357-5523
e-mail: gzenner@netins.net

APPENDIX B: Modeling Mallard Harvest Rates

We modeled harvest rates of mid-continent mallards within a Bayesian hierarchical framework. We developed a set of models to predict harvest rates under each regulatory alternative as a function of the harvest rates observed under the liberal alternative, using historical information relating harvest rates to various regulatory alternatives. We modeled the probability of regulation-specific harvest rates (h) based on normal distributions with the following parameterizations:

Closed: $\quad p(h_C) \sim N(\mu_C, v_C^2)$

Restrictive: $\quad p(h_R) \sim N(\gamma_R \mu_L, v_R^2)$

Moderate: $\quad p(h_M) \sim N(\gamma_M \mu_L + \delta_f, v_M^2)$

Liberal: $\quad p(h_L) \sim N(\mu_L + \delta_f, v_L^2)$

For the restrictive and moderate alternatives we introduced the parameter γ to represent the relative difference between the harvest rate observed under the liberal alternative and the moderate or restrictive alternatives. Based on this parameterization, we are making use of the information that has been gained (under the liberal alternative) and are modeling harvest rates for the restrictive and moderate alternatives as a function of the mean harvest rate observed under the liberal alternative. For the harvest-rate distributions assumed under the restrictive and moderate regulatory packages, we specified that γ_R and γ_M are equal to the prior estimates of the predicted mean harvest rates under the restrictive and moderate alternatives divided by the prior estimates of the predicted mean harvest rates observed under the liberal alternative. Thus, these parameters act to scale the mean of the restrictive and moderate distributions in relation to the mean harvest rate observed under the liberal regulatory alternative. We also considered the marginal effect of framework-date extensions under the moderate and liberal alternatives by including the parameter δ_f.

In order to update the probability distributions of harvest rates realized under each regulatory alternative, we first needed to specify a prior probability distribution for each of the model parameters. These distributions represent prior beliefs regarding the relationship between each regulatory alternative and the expected harvest rates. We used a normal distribution to represent the mean and a scaled inverse-chi-square distribution to represent the variance of the normal distribution of the likelihood. For the mean (μ) of each harvest-rate distribution associated with each regulatory alternative, we use the predicted mean harvest rates provided in USFWS (2000a:13-14), assuming uniformity of regulatory prescriptions across flyways. We set prior values of each standard deviation (v) equal to 20% of the mean (CV = 0.2) based on an analysis by Johnson et al. (1997). We then specified the following prior distributions and parameter values under each regulatory package:

Closed (in U.S. only):

$$p(\mu_C) \sim N(0.0088, \frac{0.0018^2}{6})$$

$$p(v_C^2) \sim Scaled\ Inv\text{-}\chi^2(6, 0.0018^2)$$

These closed-season parameter values are based on observed harvest rates in Canada during the 1988-93 seasons, which was a period of restrictive regulations in both Canada and the United States.

For the restrictive and moderate alternatives, we specified that the standard error of the normal distribution of the scaling parameter is based on a coefficient of variation for the mean equal to 0.3. The scale parameter of the inverse-chi-square distribution was set equal to the standard deviation of the harvest rate mean under the restrictive and moderate regulation alternatives (i.e., CV = 0.2).

Restrictive:

$$p(\gamma_R) \sim N(0.51, \frac{0.15^2}{6})$$

$$p(v_R^2) \sim Scaled\ Inv\text{-}\chi^2(6, 0.0133^2)$$

Moderate:

$$p(\gamma_M) \sim N(0.85, \frac{0.26^2}{6})$$

$$p(v_M^2) \sim Scaled\ Inv\text{-}\chi^2(6, 0.0223^2)$$

Liberal:

$$p(\mu_L) \sim N(0.1305, \frac{0.0261^2}{6})$$

$$p(v_L^2) \sim Scaled\ Inv\text{-}\chi^2(6, 0.0261^2)$$

The prior distribution for the marginal effect of the framework-date extension was specified as:

$$p(\delta_f) \sim N(0.02, 0.01^2)$$

The prior distributions were multiplied by the likelihood functions based on the last seven years of data under liberal regulations, and the resulting posterior distributions were evaluated with Markov Chain Monte Carlo simulation. Posterior estimates of model parameters and of annual harvest rates are provided in the following table:

Parameter	Estimate	SD	Parameter	Estimate	SD
μ_C	0.0088	0.0020	h_{1998}	0.1093	0.0114
v_C	0.0019	0.0005	h_{1999}	0.1000	0.0077
γ_R	0.5105	0.0593	h_{2000}	0.1261	0.0101
v_R	0.0128	0.0032	h_{2001}	0.1071	0.0111
γ_M	0.8501	0.1113	h_{2002}	0.1132	0.0059
v_M	0.0216	0.0054	h_{2003}	0.1131	0.0084
μ_L	0.1154	0.0071	h_{2004}	0.1245	0.0108
v_L	0.0213	0.0042	h_{2005}	0.1174	0.0082
δ_f	0.0115	0.0082			

We modeled harvest rates of eastern mallards using the same parameterizations as those for mid-continent mallards:

Closed: $\qquad p(h_C) \sim N(\mu_C, v_C^2)$

Restrictive: $\quad p(h_R) \sim N(\gamma_R \mu_L, v_R^2)$

Moderate: $\quad p(h_M) \sim N(\gamma_M \mu_L + \delta_f, v_M^2)$

Liberal: $\qquad p(h_L) \sim N(\mu_L + \delta_f, v_L^2)$

We set prior values of each standard deviation (v) equal to 30% of the mean (CV = 0.3) to account for additional variation due to changes in regulations in the other Flyways and their unpredictable effects on the harvest rates of eastern mallards. We then specified the following prior distribution and parameter values for the liberal regulatory alternative:

Liberal:

$$p(\mu_L) \sim N(0.1771, \frac{0.0531^2}{6})$$

$$p(v_L^2) \sim Scaled\ Inv\text{-}\chi^2(6, 0.0531^2)$$

Moderate:

$$p(\gamma_M) \sim N(0.92, \frac{0.28^2}{6})$$

$$p(v_M^2) \sim Scaled\ Inv\text{-}\chi^2(6, 0.0488^2)$$

Restrictive:

$$p(\gamma_R) \sim N(0.76, \frac{0.28^2}{6})$$

$$p(v_R^2) \sim Scaled\ Inv\text{-}\chi^2(6, 0.0406^2)$$

Closed (in U.S. only):

$$p(\mu_C) \sim N(0.0800, \frac{0.0240^2}{6})$$

$$p(v_C^2) \sim Scaled\ Inv\text{-}\chi^2(6, 0.0240^2)$$

A previous analysis suggested that the effect of the framework-date extension on eastern mallards would be of lower magnitude and more variable than on mid-continent mallards (USFWS 2000). Therefore, we specified the following prior distribution for the marginal effect of the framework-date extension for eastern mallards as:

$$p(\delta_f) \sim N(0.01, 0.01^2)$$

The prior distributions were multiplied by the likelihood functions based on the last four years of data under liberal regulations, and the resulting posterior distributions were evaluated with Markov Chain Monte Carlo simulation. Posterior estimates of model parameters and of annual harvest rates are provided in the following table:

Parameter	Estimate	SD	Parameter	Estimate	SD
μ_C	0.0797	0.0251	h_{2002}	0.1630	0.0129
v_C	0.0230	0.0055	h_{2003}	0.1466	0.0105
γ_R	0.7695	0.1175	h_{2004}	0.1373	0.0115
v_R	0.0392	0.0098	h_{2005}	0.1282	0.0118
γ_M	0.9074	0.1139			
v_M	0.0473	0.0119			
μ_L	0.1576	0.0169			
v_L	0.0460	0.0106			
δ_f	0.0060	0.0098